Slavery and the Slave Trade

Slavery and the Slave Trade

A Short Illustrated History

JAMES WALVIN

University Press of Mississippi
Jackson

First published in 1983 in the United States of America by the University Press of Mississippi

Second Printing 1984

Library of Congress Cataloging in Publication Data

Walvin, James.
 Slavery and the slave trade.

 Bibliography: p.
 Includes index.
 1. Slavery–History. 2. Slave-trade–History.
I. Title.
HT861.W34 1983   306′.362′09   82–24833
ISBN 0–87805–180–5
ISBN 0–87805–181–3 (pbk.)

Contents

Acknowledgements

The author and publisher wish to acknowledge the following illustration sources:

The Mansell Collection; The Mary Evans Picture Library; The British Museum; The British Library; *The Illustrated London News* 43, 71; The City of Bristol Museum and Art Gallery 59; The National Portrait Gallery 61; The Walker Art Gallery, Liverpool 62; The National Gallery of Canada, Ottawa 64.

Introduction

Many modern readers will automatically think of slavery in terms of that institution which was responsible for taking so many Africans from their homelands and using them as slaves in the Americas. The public image of slavery, conveyed by television, films and popular literature, is of a largely black phenomenon. Yet in spite of the importance of black slavery (and the bulk of this book is concerned with that particular form of slavery) it would be to distort recorded history to think of slavery uniquely in black or American terms. Forms of slavery were commonplace and ubiquitous long before the importation of black slaves into the New World. Similarly, it ought not to be thought that slavery ended when the last slave was freed in Brazil in 1888, for certain types of slavery have survived (and sometimes thrived) to the present day. Stories periodically appear in the press about the 'white slave trade', child 'slave labour' or slavery in various parts of the developing world. One difficulty in assessing these stories, however, is to know what commentators mean when they use the terms 'slaves' and 'slavery'. In fact this problem is not very different from that faced by historians when studying the history of slavery. For instance, it is extremely difficult to provide a definition of slavery which is equally applicable to all the varied historical situations where slavery existed. To put the matter crudely, an African slave in eighteenth-century Jamaica cannot easily be compared with a Roman slave or a medieval serf.

To a degree the difficulty is one of terminology. The term 'slave' has often been used very loosely to describe and to lump together many different types of non-free people. In part this has been due to the difficulties of translation; of finding suitable words for Latin and Greek categories which do not easily translate. This has led to a consequent blurring of distinctions. But it is also true that many difficulties in understanding the wider history of slavery are partly due to the fact that people in the west tend to think of slaves largely, if not solely, in terms of black slaves. In fact there is a strong case for arguing that slavery in the Americas is, in many respects, the exception and ought not to be compared with other forms of human bondage.

vii

Slaves and slave systems varied enormously. Slave experiences were incomparably different in law, social custom and economic practice, not merely between the different slave societies but sometimes even within the same society. The rights and obligations of a slave in one society might seem more like the lot of a free man in another slave society. In part, this brief history is designed to illustrate that diversity of slave experience. But it is also intended to suggest how widespread – indeed ubiquitous – was slavery in a number of societies.

It is a bold project, its ambitiousness compounded by the limitations of space and the restrictions of the author's own expertise. In the fields of classical slavery and medieval serfdom I have been guided by other people's researches and in trying to distil their complex arguments for a general readership I trust that I have not traduced their scholarship. I have benefited from the guidance and editorial comments of Barrie Dobson, Alan Hall and John Parker in those areas where I felt uncertain. Although much more familiar with the work on black slavery, even here the author faces difficulties. The subject is so vast and the literature so profuse – and expanding – that no single author can claim to be master of the total subject. It is then inevitable that my own research interests will influence the shape and direction of this book. If what follows seems to be particularly British – or British Caribbean – I trust that will in no way detract from its strengths.

If the book has one overall purpose, it is to present for a wide readership a reasonably comprehensive view of an important historical topic, drawing upon the most recent historical research and presenting it in a format that makes that research comprehensible to a non-specialised audience.

YORK,   JAMES WALVIN
APRIL 1981

1. Slavery in Antiquity

Different forms of slavery existed in numerous societies long before the rise of modern European civilisation. That civilisation was born and nurtured in the Mediterranean basin; conceived initially in Greece and later transformed and exported to an ever-widening geographical area by the expansion of the Roman Empire. This Graeco-Roman world, which lasted approximately from 1000 BC to 500 AD, developed in that time from a series of small communities into a major polity which spread itself from the Atlantic to the Caucasus and from the British Isles to the Sahara.[1] It was however an unevenly spread civilisation and those parts of its population – and cities – which mattered most skirted the Mediterranean. It was one of the major achievements of the Romans that their armies and administrators moved into the interior of Europe, Asia Minor and North Africa, forcing their reluctant (and, to the Romans, 'barbarian') peoples into a submission to the world of Rome. The resulting Roman Empire embraced a vast region whose unity existed primarily as a political unit dominated by and subservient to Rome.[2]

Both Greece and Rome were slave societies; slaves occupied a central economic and demographic role in the wider society. Yet to make this assertion is to simplify and therefore to distort remarkably complex historical situations. There were times, for instance, in the history of classical antiquity when the divide between free and enslaved was often blurred and uncertain. A large proportion of the population owned slaves, large numbers of whom were thoroughly exploited although not all by any means endured harsh or abject conditions. Many slaves were themselves prosperous; some even became eminent men. Nor was it merely the prosperous who owned slaves; we know of many cases where the very poor owned and employed slaves.

In law Greek and Roman slaves were accorded a uniform condition, but in practice they undertook a great variety of tasks and roles, 'all of which might equally be performed by dependents of free or citizen status'.[3] In domestic service they undertook the whole range of tasks of caring for their masters' and mistresses' every material and physical need.[4] Even in the hell of the silver and sulphur

1

1. A badge for a Roman slave, from the third century AD. The badge was a warrant for a slave's arrest if he ran away

mines, where working conditions were at their worst, slaves could be found at work alongside freemen and condemned criminals.[5]

Greek and Roman commentators tended to divide mankind into free and slave; but in fact there were a number of other groups who occupied the middle ground, who were neither free nor yet slaves. But such people were nonetheless securely bound to masters or to the state. Chattel slavery, where the slave was regarded and treated as a thing, to be purchased and sold like any other item of property, was indeed common from at least 500 BC. But there were also large numbers of people who were dependent and whose exact status is difficult to define and describe. To a degree this is because of the shortcomings of our own language and terminology. There is no modern term which adequately describes those people subjected to debt-bondage or those who were semi-servile *coloni*. Greeks and Romans, like many modern historians, found it easier to describe such people as slaves. Yet until roughly the sixth century BC in Greece, and from the third century BC in Rome, such semi-servile people may have been more widespread and important than chattel slavery itself. In time, however, chattel slavery emerged as a central institution in both Greece and Rome, evolving primarily because of fundamental economic changes in society at large. These changes rendered the older bonded or dependent workers less important and as the old labour systems proved unsatisfactory, a starker form of slavery was slowly established. In its initial stages it was possible to introduce slavery by importation of captured peoples from the peripheries of Greece and Rome.[6] As trade and empire grew it became progressively easier to recruit – by war, piracy and general physical superiority – captive outsiders who were imported to work as slaves.

It is impossible to know with any precision the numbers of slaves to be found in classical Greece; historians have offered estimates ranging from 20,000 to 400,000.[7] We depend upon tantalising fragments of evidence which provide information that is revealing if nonetheless inconclusive. Thucydides records that in 413 BC more than 20,000 Athenian slaves, the majority of whom were craftsmen, deserted to the besieging Spartans.[8] It is easier to describe what slaves did. Slaves were widely used as domestic servants (where they had the additional advantage of conferring status upon their owner). In Greece they undertook work on the land, in industries and the crafts. Xenophon wrote, 'Those who can do so buy slaves to share their work with them'[9] and it seems to have been common for craftsmen to use slaves, train them in artisanal skills hoping eventually to be able to retire and to live upon the proceeds of their slaves' labour. Socrates tells of a miller, a baker and clothier, all of whom were able to live in comfort on the efforts of their slaves.[10] As we might expect in a society which was, by modern standards, small-scale and dependent on artisans rather than large-scale industry, such slaves generally lived and worked in small units. There were exceptions however. We know of one man alone who employed thirty-two slaves as cutlers and twenty as bedmakers. Two brothers employed 120 slaves as shield-makers in what was the largest (and therefore exceptional) industrial enterprise. We also know of Nikias who owned 1000 slaves working in the silver mines.[11]

It is abundantly clear that many of the highly specialised skills displayed in surviving architectural and creative artefacts were the works of slaves as well as free men. Among slaves were flute girls and harpists while auction lists reveal a goldsmith, fabric-maker, spit-maker and a cobbler. Those slaves with the rarer skills received higher pay for their work and their owners could expect to receive a higher price for them at sales.[12]

The large-scale holdings of slaves, so common centuries later in the American colonies, were perhaps less common in antiquity. There were, it is true, exceptions to this rule, notably in the silver mines where, according to Xenophon, some 10,000 were employed.[13] Similarly, large gangs of slaves were to be found in Roman agriculture. In general, however, slaves were not to be found in such large concentrations. They were more commonly to be found in domestic work; it has been calculated that one-half of the entire Greek slave population was employed as servants. The lot of domestic servants varied a great deal and much depended upon the particular master or mistress. A cruel or vindictive owner could make life intolerable. On the other hand, at its best the slave's relationship with an owner might be friendly or benign. Good relations and faithful service might, for instance, lead to eventual freedom for the slave, a recurring feature throughout the subsequent history of successive forms of slavery; loyalty and good service could lead to gratitude and gratefulness and even to freedom. Some slaves were able to purchase their own freedom, though in Athens manumission rarely conferred the full rights of citizenship.[14] Familiarity with black slavery might persuade us to think of slavery as unpaid, yet in classical Greece slaves were often paid for their work. Even those slaves who lived apart from their owners might be able to earn enough eventually to secure their own freedom.[15] Certain Athenian slaves were even able to attain a marked degree of prosperity.[16] We need, however, to recall the opposite and contrasting situations; of domestic slaves cowed and tied to harsh and hostile owners and having few prospects other than an unhappy and unremitting lifetime's bondage. However they were treated (and it clearly varied enormously) it was these domestic slaves who enabled the free Athenians – like the whites in the slave colonies of the New World – to pursue their business and to enjoy their social lives so fully. Slaves were instrumental, but not always uniquely responsible, for enhancing their owners' economic wellbeing and their leisure lives.

It should now be clear that the slaves' conditions varied greatly within Athens and between the different city states. In Spartan-controlled territory, the helots, who greatly outnumbered their Spartan masters, were generally regarded and designated as slaves. Yet their status was quite distinct from the slaves of Athens. Helots were not free but nor were they owned by individuals; they could not be freed, bought or sold. Moreover, they formed a self-perpetuating group whereas slaves were recruited both by birth and importation.[17] The helots formed a large, coherent and, for the same reasons, a potentially rebellious group. The helots, unlike the slaves in classical Greece, revolted against their masters.[18] Spartan society lived in perpetual fear and danger from the helots just as the planters of the New World were to live in perpetual fear of their slaves. Spartans, like those planters, took great pains to keep potential weapons out of the hands of their helots and, again like the planters, they also took the wise precaution of arming themselves.[19] The helots were obviously a group whose servile and threatening presence would have proved uncomfortably familiar to slave holders in the Americas.

Both Greeks and Romans tended increasingly to divide up mankind into two main groups: themselves and others. The Greek city states, like the Romans later, regarded the rest of mankind as inferior and barbarian. And it was from among these outsiders, conquered and captured, that the Greeks found a plentiful supply of slaves. Apart from a debate which took place during the fourth century BC, the aftermath of which we hear occasional echoes, it seems that few voices were raised against slavery during antiquity. Throughout most of recorded western history, from classical antiquity to the present, the general view was that slavery and other forms of bondage were natural, unquestioned and important for a host of reasons. Slavery was assumed to be natural, as Aristotle argued:

> Therefore all men who differ from one another by as much as the soul differs from the body or man from a wild beast (and that is the state of those who work by using their bodies, and for whom that is the best they can do) – these people are slaves by nature, and it is better for them to be subject to this kind of control, as it is better for the other creatures I have mentioned. For a man who is able to belong to another person is by nature a slave.[20]

Like the Greeks before them, the Romans developed a complex system of slavery. For six centuries (200 BC to 500 AD) the Roman Empire extended itself around the Mediterranean and across Europe. Rome, the centre of this unparalleled empire, became the largest city in the world with a population of one million. And from this centre an imperial system developed which transformed the nature and economy of Italy and subjugated Europe into political and economic dependence on Rome. As the city of Rome itself grew it became a major task simply to feed the Roman people. To do so, agriculture throughout the region was transformed and in the process slaves to work the land came to be used with growing frequency. In this economic transformation two related features were paramount: the growing wealth of the Roman elite and the prodigious numerical growth of the slave community.[21] By the time of Christ, there were perhaps two to three million slaves in Italy, forming between 35–40 per cent of the total population; a higher ratio of slave to free than was later to be found in slave society in the US South.[22] Moreover, among the agricultural slaves men were in a majority.[23] This massive slave population owed its origins directly to

2. A Roman slave market, by Boulanger

two centuries of successful warfare through which Rome conquered much of the Mediterranean region and was able to draw off vast wealth from the subjugated area. They also captured hundreds of thousands of prisoners. These prisoners of war formed a standard source of Roman slaves, large numbers of whom were set to a life of labour on the land, a process which further enhanced the wealth of Rome.

When a Roman general returned to the capital in triumph, his victims and prisoners were symbolically driven before him in triumphant procession through the streets of Rome. They were both prisoners and slaves and throughout these centuries of Roman ascendancy, these processions became a frequent and well-publicised ceremony.[24] From this same military success and the consolidation of empire, the Roman elite made great financial gains which were invested in expanding their rural estates. Just as many of these large estates were a result of war, yet another by-product of military action – the slaves – were used to work the land. Thus, newly expanded land and slave labour went together, in much the same fashion that was to become familiar in the tropical Americas centuries later. Slaves became a major and vital force in the consolidation of Roman wealth and were crucial in the major task of

3. Slaves attending their owner in a draper's shop, second century AD

feeding the urban people of Rome. Large numbers of slaves could also be found in the crafts and industries and working for and waiting upon the domestic needs of their conquerors and owners.

In many respects, slavery in Rome has seemed (to historians if rarely to contemporary slave owners) an inefficient and uneconomic system. Before the importation of slaves Roman agriculture had managed reasonably well, using a free peasantry on smaller land-ownings. But in a society which needed ever more men for periods of lengthy military service throughout the empire, the peasantry was effectively reduced under a crippling burden of military service. Slaves, on the other hand – and for obvious reasons – could not be drained away to fight imperial wars. Though sullen, costly and less than keen, the slaves were nonetheless completely at their owners' beck and call. Above all else it was perhaps the malleability of the slave labour force which made it so attractive to its owners. Slaves could be herded together or divided up into work gangs, a process which would have been inappropriate or unacceptable to free labour. And, in the process, as Roman slaves became the foundation of Roman agriculture, they also became part of the land itself; to be sold, like the animals and the buildings, along with the estate. Purchasers had no trouble in finding labour to work their lands for the two went together. Furthermore, once slavery had substantially insinuated itself into the rural Italian economy it developed an economic logic of its own. Rural slave owners became wedded to the belief that slavery was indispensable to their wellbeing.

The existence of slavery in Rome had important political repercussions, not least for the impoverished but free element in Roman society who, however abject their circumstances, could always take comfort from the fact that they occupied a superior position to the slaves. In a society where status and the esteem of others counted for much, the certainty among the poor that beneath them lay a mass of exploited slaves was a comforting thought; an ingredient in establishing political stability. But there was a reverse side to this coin, namely the discontent among the slaves. The Romans had a proverb which warned 'Every slave is an enemy'.[25] It was an aphorism born of social reality. Viewing the slaves as potential enemies inevitably led to cruelty and ill-treatment and while some laws sought to protect the slaves from the cruelty of owners, in general the law was powerless to prevent the worst excesses which were endemic on large-scale slave holdings and which often stemmed not so much from wanton cruelty, but from the sheer oppression and arduousness of difficult labour.

Slave revolts remained a perennial threat, not surprisingly perhaps in the light of the high proportion of slaves in society at large. Between 134–2 BC Sicily was wracked by slave revolts, but it was the Spartacus revolt of 73–1 BC which remains the best remembered of slave uprisings. The causes of the slave revolts were complex. Often, the introduction of large numbers of new slaves (people who had once been free but who now found themselves enslaved by acts of conquest) into harsh working and living conditions was a crucial factor. Similarly in the New World, imported Africans and not the locally born (or Creole) slaves tended to be the customary instigators of black revolts. There were, however, other factors which could spark off servile revolt. In Sicily, for instance, rural slaves were allowed a marked degree of freedom – in order to provide themselves with food and clothing – while in the towns many slaves mixed freely with free people, in the process imbibing dangerous ideas and disruptive notions.[26] In Sicily the slave revolts seem to have been encouraged by the enforced resettlement of slaves and the presence of armed and unsupervised herdsmen, at a time when local political feuds enfeebled government control over its subject people thus unconsciously providing the slaves with the opportunity to organise and resist. In the case of Spartacus, the initial insurgents, having been trained as gladiators, were well equipped to organise and to lead a revolt. Around the leadership of Spartacus and his fellow gladiators there quickly developed a slave army able to fight the professional legions of the Roman army. The slaves wanted to secure their freedom and to be repatriated to their homelands. In taking up arms against their masters, however, they knew that they faced stark alternatives: success or a horrifying fate at the hands of vengeful slave owners. Thus the Spartacus cause was desperate and the fighting savage. Faced with defeat, rebellious slaves often preferred suicide or death at the hands of a comrade, to Roman punishments. In this there is a parallel with many of the slave revolts in the Americas or on the slave ships so many centuries later. When the rebellion of Spartacus was finally crushed, 6000 crucified slaves lined the road from Capua to Rome; a grotesque reminder to all who saw it and to those who merely heard about it of the futility of revolt and of the inevitable fate which awaited insurgent slaves.[27]

For all their savagery, slave revolts were unusual although slaves were able to resist in a number of different ways. Open revolt was only the most desperate and in many respects hopeless tilt at their masters. Among Roman slaves (and later among Afro-American slaves) the most common form of slave resistance 'took the form of guile, lying and indolence'.[28] Slave holders could be hurt in a myriad of ways short of open revolt. But it would be foolish to pretend that the ultimate victims of Roman slavery were any other than the millions of slaves themselves. Slaves' lives were all too often the playthings of capricious owners, and the slaves' wellbeing and sometimes even their very existence was dependent on accident or fate. In its most extreme form *all* slaves of a slave owner murdered by a slave were themselves to be tortured and killed. In an exceptional, though nonetheless real case, 400 household slaves were slaughtered for that reason. Intimidation in life and the ever-present threat of death were regarded as invaluable elements in overawing this potentially dangerous body of slaves:

so long as our slaves act as informers, we may live in a minority amid the mass, secure while they fear, and finally, if we die, certain of vengeance against the guilty.

Tactitus, who recorded the Senate debate on the case of the 400 executed slaves, reported:

Now that our households comprise tribes with customs the opposite of our own, with strange cults or none, you will never coerce such a mixture of humanity, except by terror.[29]

A central dilemma of a slave society – or rather of its ruling master class – continued to be how best to govern the slaves. Too liberal or lax a hand seemed no less dangerous than the harshest of repressions. In truth, as Romans (and, later, Caribbean planters) discovered, there was no ideal policy for managing slaves, for each approach contained its own shortcomings and the seeds of its own failures. The prime motivation was economic, namely to exact the best returns from enslaved labour. Yet the dictates of economics might not always coincide with the best interests of security and good social order. There were, it is true, large numbers of laws designed to protect the Roman slave and, at first glance, these laws seem enlightened and reasonable. Like so many laws, however, they sometimes provide little or no guide to social reality and it has been noted that 'laws and social values deprecating cruelty failed to prevent excesses'.[30] For every liberal, legal pronouncement, the cynical observer could point to many more acts of tyranny against the slaves.

Roman slaves could however take advantage of certain features of contemporary bondage. Unlike black slaves later, the Roman slaves had no distinguishing features. Suggestions to make them wear common clothing were rejected for fear of encouraging a sense of self-importance and collective strength.[31] Furthermore, substantial numbers of Roman slaves were able to secure their freedom. It could be argued that the prospects of manumission – of working hard to save enough money to buy it or being sufficiently loyal to earn it – represents an important safety valve for the slave system. Equally, however, manumission represented an economic decision on the part of the slave owner; at what point could the owner afford to release a slave from bondage? Whatever the reason, the freeing of Roman slaves was common. Two thousand years later, in the black slave societies of the New World, it was much less common. Roman statistics are hard to come by but the general impression is firm enough. In Rome itself, a substantial proportion of the population consisted of ex-slaves. One man alone was estimated to have freed 10,000. The Roman fire brigade, 7000 strong, was recruited from ex-slaves. Indeed a law was passed preventing slave owners from manumitting more than 100 slaves in their wills.[32] But many slaves were freed in their masters' lifetime. Among skilled – and therefore valuable – slaves it is likely that this prospect of freedom was an important incentive to work industriously and honestly.

The evidence suggests that substantial numbers of slaves were liberated partially or unconditionally by their owners. Furthermore, it is apparent that many slaves paid substantial amounts for their freedom: a clear indication of the savings possible for certain slaves. But such voluntary manumission did not play a part in the ending of

Roman slavery. Slavery did not disappear, nor was it abolished, but it became less and less important. The decline of Roman slavery was partly related to the sheer size of the empire and the cost of transporting captured slaves. The decline was not directly related to the rise of Christianity. On the contrary, it was a Christian emperor, Justinian, who codified the slave laws and, unconsciously, provided Europeans 'with a ready-made legal foundation for the slavery they introduced into the New World a thousand years later'.[33] It is much more likely that the decline of slavery was set in train by a complex long-term economic transformation. Employers of labour, particularly on the land, had no need to turn to slaves from the far reaches of the empire since a plentiful and depressed labour force became available locally. To the lands once worked by slaves, free tenants were gradually introduced. Ironically perhaps, the freedom of these labourers was itself eroded as they became ever more firmly tied to the lands they worked. They were bonded and obligated – but nonetheless free. In the process, slavery itself withered away as its former economic importance declined, though pockets of slavery could still be found scattered round the empire long after it had died at the centre.

It would be pointless to make moral judgements about slavery in antiquity. The fact that slavery offends modern sensibilities ought not to persuade us that it was similarly offensive in older societies. It is true that in both Greece and Rome a number of moral and philosophical criticisms were levelled at slavery, but such views were unusual and, as far as we can judge, only marginal. Contemporaries judged slavery on the value, importance and distinctiveness of the work the slaves performed. This is not to say that classical slavery can be assessed uniquely in economic terms, for it is also true that slavery was sometimes able to survive *despite* its economic shortcomings. In Greece and Rome it was a highly successful system which lasted for centuries – far longer in fact than modern freedoms and political democracy have existed in the west. For generations of Athenians and Romans, slavery was an inherited and unquestioned fact of life; an institution which had, since time out of mind, helped their state and its citizens to prosper. Throughout much of its history, classical slavery was then unquestioned, on moral or economic grounds. It thrived on the movement of empire; on military successes which yielded booty, wealth and supplies of slaves. Greek and Roman conquests were crucial determinants of slavery, draining the borderlands of the empire of untold armies of people in order to feed the appetite of the imperial heartland for rural labour, domestic service and a range of industrial and labouring skills.

Slavery thrived in the Mediterranean region and Europe for a thousand years. By contrast, slavery throughout the Americas lasted for less than half that period. If longevity and durability offer some indication of success, then classical slavery was clearly to be counted successful, more so perhaps than any other known slave system. It is of course less well known because it is so distant and because the evidence is so fragmented and often disputed. Moreover, the slave systems which emerged in more recent, and better-documented, eras have tended to overshadow classical slavery. Yet it is important to recall that Graeco-Roman civilisation – the foundation of western civilisation – was, no less than the later plantation colonies, a slave society.

2. Slaves and Serfs

There was nothing to compare with the institution of Roman slavery – in size, scope and nature – until the evolution of black slavery in the New World. But this is not to claim that, in the intervening millenium which separated the decline of Rome from the European settlement of the Americas, slavery was unknown. On the contrary, it was commonplace throughout western Europe. But there was no western slave society as such; none in which slavery occupied a central position in the economic and demographic make-up of society at large. Slavery was commonplace but peripheral. Slave trading continued and would do so as long as people fell victim to conquerors who could profit from selling their captives. We know of a slave market at Verdun in the seventh century. It was usual, for instance, for prisoners of war when not put to death to be sold into slavery, a widespread practice throughout the Viking period of the ninth and tenth centuries. As the Vikings swept across northern Europe conquering and establishing a complex and far-reaching web of trading links, many of their subject peoples were enslaved and sold throughout Europe's slave markets. There was, furthermore, a thriving slave trade from northern Europe to North Africa, and for centuries after the collapse of Roman authority a European slave-trading system survived which sought to satisfy the demand for slaves from Islamic Spain and North Africa.[1] Slaves travelled over the Brenner Pass to Venice, to be shipped into Islam. Indeed much of the valuable coinage and precious metals which found its way to Viking Scandinavia was payment for the slaves shipped south.[2]

Anglo-Saxon England, like its European neighbours, was a slave-holding community although it was far from being a slave society in any meaningful sense of the word. It is possible that there were large numbers of slaves in England in the seventh and eighth centuries. But whatever position slaves occupied in Anglo-Saxon England it was, like so many other features of society, disrupted and altered by the impact of the Norman Conquest. While Norman England itself was not characterised by slavery it would clearly be wrong to view it as a society where freedom predominated, for under the Normans and subsequent early medieval monarchs England had a largely

13

servile population which had little semblance of personal or
collective freedoms. And that was true of much of contemporary
Europe where the bulk of the population, if not enslaved, was
certainly less than free.

It seems likely that the very great majority of the people of
medieval Europe were, in some degree or other, unfree. Of course
lack of freedom (today as then) takes a great variety of forms and
may, at its simplest, result merely from abject poverty. But the lack
of freedom in medieval Europe was more than this for the structure
of law and government were specifically designed to institutionalise
and support the limits on freedom. The bulk of the European
population were peasants who shared, despite a great number of
local variations and peculiarities, a servile status which was
hereditary. These were the serfs who were tied to the land by a series
of onerous obligations to their masters. It may seem merely a
semantic point to draw a distinction between slave and serf but we
need to recall that it was a distinction which was well known,
important and obvious to contemporaries. In general, the slave – in
antiquity and in Europe of the so-called 'Dark Ages' – was a thing, a
chattel and a piece of property. By definition the slave owned
nothing and the fact that, in practice, slaves in antiquity and the
early middle ages, by dint of good fortune, sympathetic owners or
hard work, were able to accumulate material possessions does not
undermine this legal status. As a 'thing' the slave was legally denied
the rights of ownership. Serfs had at their disposal the means of
producing their own livelihood. As working peasants they
controlled, but they did not own, the material implements needed in
agriculture. Their tools, buildings and substantial parts of the goods
they produced or grew belonged not to them but to the land-owner.
Serfs were tied to the land from one generation to another just as
surely as they were tied to an endless back-breaking routine of harsh
work in order simply to survive. Yet medieval serfs, for all their lack
of mobility, the weight of their inherited obligations and the
commonplace misery of their lives, were not slaves – and few
thought of them as such.

The differences between serfs and slaves become even more
confused when we recall that in material terms the slave might enjoy
much superior conditions to the serf. Although it was common, it
was not axiomatic that the material lot of a slave should be the most
abject of all. As we have seen, there were slaves in Athens and Rome
who progressed to positions of rank and social esteem and who
accumulated a degree of material wealth which would have been the
envy of a medieval serf. Similarly, towards the end of black slavery
in the Americas there were critics who argued that West Indian and

American slaves enjoyed material conditions superior to those of contemporary European (notably Irish) peasants. We must not assume, however, that material conditions determine or shape the nature of human bondage. However prosperous a slave might have been he was, for all that, a slave. Conversely, however prosperous or miserable a serf, he was not a slave. Serfdom was nonetheless a condition of bondage – a condition of man which was characterised, indeed defined, by its lack of freedoms.

The serfs of medieval Europe had emerged as a group – perhaps even as a class – in a number of different ways. Some were descended from the *coloni* of the late Empire, driven into progressive serfdom by a growing accumulation of debts or obligations to land-owners.[3] Other serfs were the direct descendants of slaves, while still others had come from the world of free men – a decline whose descent was often brought about by a growing number of dues to land-owners. There were others too who had even voluntarily become serfs in order to stake a claim to the land. Freedom without the ability to provide for oneself and one's family was not necessarily prized above all else; above, for instance, the simple need to keep body and soul together.[4] We must not imagine that medieval people valued the abstract principles which the modern reader might think essential.

Across large tracts of the former Roman Empire, there was a noticeable process of enserfment at work, especially after the ninth century. It was naturally a complex process at the heart of which lay major economic change. In the case of England it is possible to trace the development and nature of servitude with some precision because, following the Norman Conquest, the Domesday Book of 1086 provides a remarkable analysis of the population. Some 9 per cent of the people described in that book were categorised as slaves, though in certain parts of the country it could be as high as 20 per cent.[5] The process of reorganisation, of land-holding, administration and even of loyalties, set in train after 1066 by William I, was to transform the face of the conquered land. In the process it became unique among European nations in the sheer strength acquired by the state. The Norman state in England was, by contemporary European standards, unusually strong and the monarch was able to exact a range of commitments and loyalties from all subjects. By distributing some 5000 fiefs through the country, William I hoped to hold down the country by creating a complex pyramid of contractual loyalties, all focusing on his own kingly power – and that power ultimately derived from his award of land.[6] There thus developed not merely the most consolidated state in western Europe but, to support it, a manorial system (evidence for

4. Peasants planting seeds, from a fifteenth-century Book of Hours

which can be found *before* 1066) more advanced in the south than elsewhere, which depended for its efficacy on tight control and exploitation. This in its turn produced 'an intensification of labour services and a marked degradation of the local peasantry'.[7] Over the next century the English peasants found themselves increasingly bowed down by onerous and efficiently managed demands of the new manorial system. There ensued a widening process of enserfment which drew to itself more and more peasants, so that whatever the legal distinctions, the different gradations within the plebeian population became blurred and the observers became aware of a single class of serfs. By the twelfth century the English serf was the dominant – though dominated – social group at the lower reaches of the English social structure. Set against this process of enserfment it is true that there also developed a remarkable and distinctive structure of royal justice – though with obvious shortcomings. But this was, by and large, an abstraction which rarely altered or alleviated the miserable lot of England's serfs.

Although historians often speak of 'feudal' Europe, we need to recall that feudalism varied enormously between the different regions. It took different shape and development in, for instance, England, Germany, Italy, Spain, Portugal and Scandinavia. Yet for all these undoubted variations, feudalism was dependent upon a servile population. Moreover, it was a remarkably efficient economic and political system which mastered the agricultural environment – for which purpose, in large measure, the system was devised – more effectively perhaps than any previous system. But at the heart of feudalism lay an inevitable and conflicting clash of interests; a division between the lords who owned the lands and the servile peasants who worked it. As feudalism evolved, the serfs had slowly yet irresistibly succumbed to a growing burden of obligations. The medieval peasants lived out a recurring and apparently endless cycle of obligations to masters and land-owners: labour dues, payments in kind and in produce from the land and, of course, the obligations of loyalty. In their spare time they could cultivate the lands allocated to them – but lands which were not their own. In outline, if not in law, it was a pattern of oppression which looks remarkably similar to the lot of many black slaves in the Americas at a later date. A Bishop of Lao, writing in 1025, commented thus:

> The other class is that of the serfs, a miserable race which owns nothing that it does not get by its own labour. Who can calculate the toil by which the serfs are absorbed? Their long journeys, their labours? Money, clothing and food – all are provided by the serfs. Not one man could live without them.[8]

This could quite easily have been an uncanny description of the slaves who were to populate the slave societies of the New World, and it is a comment which gives us some indication of the similarities in kind between the medieval serf and the black slave.

Just as serfdom differed between the various parts of Europe, so too did it embrace a multitude of forms and shapes in any one country or region. Indeed the dividing line between freemen and serfs is often so blurred and confusing as to be an issue of major dispute among historians. According to Rodney Hilton, the serfs were those who were dependent on other men, were tenants of land they did not own and, in addition, 'were restricted by law in various ways as to freedom of movement, freedom to buy and sell land and goods, freedom to dispose of their own labour, freedom to marry and found a family, and freedom to leave property to their heirs'.[9] It ought not to be imagined, however, that the pre-eminence of serfdom in medieval Europe had produced the utter disappearance of slavery itself. As long as societies on the edges of Europe tolerated or used slaves, there would inevitably be a degree of European enslavement and slave trading. But the religious prohibitions against Christians enslaving other Christians became increasingly effective, especially in northern Europe. This, in conjunction with the rise of an enserfed population, ensured that slavery withered to an insignificant position. The notable exception to this pattern was the survival of domestic slavery in Italian cities. There a great deal of household activity was undertaken by Islamic or 'pagan' slaves who were imported across the Mediterranean.[10] Yet it is surely significant that when slaves were freed they generally became, not free men, but serfs. Serfdom in the words of Rodney Hilton was a ' "step up" from slavery'.[11] Equally, the voluminous English archives from the 1190s onwards give very few examples of absolute chattel slaves.

It is perhaps natural and understandable that the harshness of feudal society occasionally led to outbursts of individual or collective anger and frustration on the part of the serfs. To modern eyes it may even seem inevitable that such servile discontents would fracture the tightly controlled structure of the medieval system. Yet this would be a false and retrospective presumption. It is true that there were specifically local or personal outbursts; manifestations of grievances against a particular lord, a law or merely an individual reaction. But the history of serfdom was marked by resistance to it by serfs who found themselves to be the collective victims of harsh and often deteriorating circumstances. From the thirteenth to the fifteenth centuries there were peasant revolts of varying degrees of ferocity and effectiveness in Italy, Flanders, France, Catalonia, England and Germany.[12] The English Peasants' Revolt of 1381 was at once unique, and yet instructive of wider social grievances. This like other such revolts enshrined the demand on the part of the peasants that they ought to be free and not enserfed.[13] We know, of course, that this demand was very swiftly rebuffed in a bloody and vengeful response by king and land-owners, whose system and economic position were so threatened by the revolt and its attendant demands. Yet serfdom was in decline and the Revolt may itself, paradoxically, have been a symptom of that decline.[14]

As we shall see, slavery in the Americas was ended, in different countries, in a relatively brief period, often as a result of legislation (though this is not to deny that such legislation had a long and complex gestation period). Serfdom, on the other hand, was a much less 'artificial' system than black slavery; it was not as specifically called into being by economic interest groups. Whereas black slavery developed quickly, in response to new and specific demands, medieval serfdom evolved slowly, adapting and changing its local contours to the complex pressures exerted by existing political and economic forces. It was then quite natural that serfdom ended as it began; gradually and in piecemeal fashion. Indeed it is symptomatic that historians speak of the 'decline' of serfdom and that this decline, like serfdom's origins, is shrouded in uncertainty and historical dispute.

In the decline of serfdom perhaps the most important factor we need to consider is the Black Death and its demographic ravages in fourteenth-century Europe. The catastrophic loss of life – upwards of one-third of the population – proved to be a solvent of many of the bonds which held together the social order and at the heart of which lay serfdom. The loss of life accentuated the demand for labour and as rural population became more mobile (to satisfy that demand), the drifting away of the labour force began to weaken the traditional controls exercised by land-owners. Peasants moved from the land to find paid labour elsewhere, often in the towns whose industries began to lure the rural worker (a pattern much more familiar perhaps in the nineteenth and twentieth centuries). Faced with a loss of labour land-owners veered towards repressive insistence on their feudal rights: a tactic which in general yielded no practical results, except further to exacerbate the antagonisms of the peasants. More often, however, the land-owners were obliged to concede to the drift of events and began to compete for scarce agricultural labour by offering competitive wages and conditions – notwithstanding local and regional variations – undermining the traditional shape and structure of villeinage itself. Rents and leases gradually replaced the tying of peasants to the soil just as wages replaced their labour services. Many land-owners hastened this decline simply by manumitting – freeing – their serfs for cash. If this had the advantage of yielding quick financial returns, it had the long-term drawback of permanently removing the labourer from the land-owners' future control. The end result was that it became increasingly difficult in practice, and in law, to distinguish between the serf and the non-serf. By the early sixteenth century, the complex and protracted process had hastened the withering of serfdom as the central social and economic institution of English rural life.

In sixteenth-century England it had become an article of faith among contemporary commentators that freedom and not bondage was the distinguishing hallmark of their society. To suggest otherwise was to insult the Elizabethan belief in the unusual freedoms which they thought characterised English society. Writing about England in 1577, William Harrison noted:

> As for slaves and bondmen we have none; nay such is the privilege of our country by the special grace of God and the bounty of our princes, that if any come hither from other realms, as soon as they set foot on land they become so free of condition as their masters, whereby all note of servile bondage is utterly removed from them.[15]

Almost precisely the same view was to be repeated time and again in the next two-and-a-half centuries when Englishmen, faced by black slaves in England, took refuge in the conviction that freedom and not bondage was the natural and sanctified lot of all inhabitants of England. Yet, allowing this to be true, it represents a marked and striking contrast to the many centuries of recorded history when forms of bondage, notably serfdom, had been the foundation of English and European society. Moreover, it needs to be stressed that at the very time English serfdom came slowly to an end, its counterpart in eastern Europe was being strengthened. The decline of feudalism in western Europe was, paradoxically, paralleled by its revival throughout Europe east of the Elbe where the grain-producing territories demanded a large subject labour force. Indeed we need to remember that the Russian serfs were not emancipated until 1861, three decades after the freeing of British slaves – a reminder of the durability and longevity of European bondage. To many western Europeans as late as the eighteenth century there seemed little distinction between contemporary slavery in the New World and serfdom in eastern Europe. When Adam Smith wrote of serfdom he remarked, 'This species of slavery still subsists in Russia, Poland, Hungary, Bohemia, Moravia, and other parts of Germany.'[16]

By the mid-seventeenth century, the very time when black slavery was emerging as a major economic institution in the Americas, it is estimated that about 50 per cent of Europe's peasants were serfs, the great majority of them in the east.[17] It seems generally true that serfdom in its harshest form was to be found in Russia. There the treatment, employment, bartering and sale of serfs (independent of the land) seems very little different from the treatment accorded in law and practice to many black slaves in the Americas. Moreover,

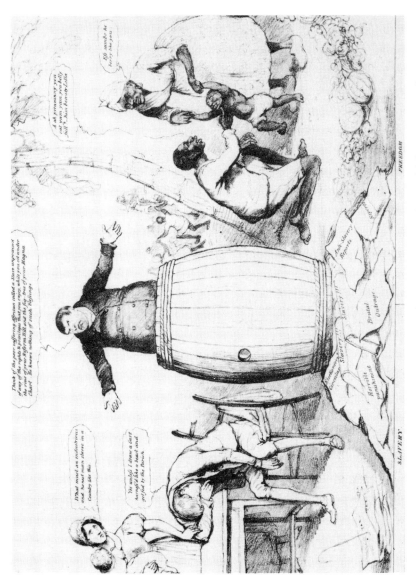

6. Cartoon from *The Looking Glass* (1832), comparing British poverty and West Indian slavery

eighteenth century.[19] It is then of great significance that one of the achievements of the French Revolution was to sweep away the last vestiges of the old feudal order by the abolition of serfdom.

The emergence of a free peasantry ought not to persuade us that this invariably led to material improvement. So much had been clear in England since the effective end of serfdom in the sixteenth century. From then onwards, and certainly until the nineteenth century, the English peasants were tied by economic circumstance, if not by feudal dues, to a land-holding class (which was increasingly capitalist) and to an unrewarding and insecure routine of life which left them to endure an impoverished freedom. A mere glance at the early nineteenth-century peasantry provides an antidote to any belief that freedom is necessarily to be equated with material improvement. It is significant that in the 1820s and 1830s the lot of the Irish peasants was frequently compared – unfavourably – with contemporary slave conditions in the British Caribbean.

From the fifteenth century onwards the English land-owning class was never again able to exercise its former feudal control over its rural labour force. But it did not need to. Henceforth it had the equally effective forces of the free market at its disposal to threaten and cajole its labour force into the required compliance and effort. If in juridicial and philosophical terms English serfdom was replaced by a free peasantry, it nevertheless remains true that the agricultural labour force remained effectively tied to the land and cowed, not by obligations, but by poverty.

Again, the parallels with black slavery are remarkable. Black peasants in the nineteenth-century Caribbean and poor black share-croppers in the post-bellum US South were often no less wretched than their slave ancestors. In all these cases it seems clear that freedom heralded not an enhancement of the material quality of life, but a continuation of abject economic conditions. Yet it is a powerful indication of the commitment to freedom that, overwhelmingly, it was sought, welcomed and clung to *despite* its attendant hardships. If people's expectations of freedom were minimal and then disappointed, rural people were unwilling to renounce it for the even more hated bondage which had characterised the lives of their forebears since time out of mind.

3. The Age of Discovery

At much the same time serfdom was in its last phases in England, the emergent capitalist classes in a number of European states, encouraged and guided by local royalty, sought an outlet for their economic interests in new and far-flung regions of the world. There was nothing new about European maritime trade, but previously most of it had been kept firmly within the geographical limits of the European coastline and the Mediterranean region, though there were major forays overland to the far (and often unknown) reaches of the world. But in the fifteenth and sixteenth centuries European merchants and adventurers broke through the traditional barriers which had so restricted them to the known world, and then began to sail to unknown and unimaginable quarters. There they traded, settled, developed local resources and returned to Europe with tales of the human and natural realities of the world at large and, perhaps most important of all, with tangible material returns on their risk and daring. They went in search of wealth, though often too they were propelled by religious zeal. Europeans had long known of the exotic produce from the East which had come overland – and of the apparently spare land begging to be acquired by the enterprising and the daring. These and other tempting items could be gained while pursuing religious ends; converting the heathens or pre-empting religious opponents, all of which gave added stimulus to the European urge to explorations. The general urge was heightened further by the fall of Constantinople to the Turks in 1453. Infidels had not merely cut the traditional routes to the East, but were now an active threat to Christian Europe. With Italy in disarray (parts actually falling to the Turks) the burden of the defence of Christian Europe fell to Castille and Portugal, whose rulers undertook a crusade against the Moslems in Spain and North Africa. One ploy of the Portuguese was to seek a route south and along the West African coastline in the hope of finding a weakness in the defences of Islam. At precisely the same time, the Spaniards, through the efforts of Columbus, had 'discovered' the New World – again in the expectation of finding a route to the East.

On the African coast, in Central America and Mexico, the

Iberians discovered local people who seemed ideally suited for religious conversion. 'Savage' even when docile, the people of the Americas and Africa swiftly fell victim to the superior technical and organisational skills of the marauding Europeans. They fell victim, in horrifying numbers, to the white man's diseases. The explorers – the *conquistadores* – were not merely privateers. On the contrary, they were often men of learning and sophistication, steeped in Renaissance learning and familiar with recent advances in the sciences, cartography and navigation. On their return they published accounts of their travels and adventures thus sharpening the educated European curiosity for even more news and evidence of life on the wider reaches of the Atlantic. Similarly the stories, and the verbal reports in the seafaring communities, whetted the appetite of other Europeans who saw in the Iberians' probes, opportunities to further their own economic (or national) interests.[1]

Many of the initial, accidental discoveries proved to be of lasting and material value. The Europeans discovered Brazil in 1500 (by a fleet bound for India) and close contacts fostered in the various parts of West Africa, either in search of local valuables (notably gold and ivory) or *en route* in search of yet another alternative path to the East. But it was eventually black inhabitants who were to prove the most attractive and valuable of local commodities. In the Americas above all there were revealed the vast expanses of land and islands which were to lure Europeans across the Atlantic throughout the ensuing centuries. Changing circumstances were to fuse together these two utterly unrelated factors – land in the New World and African labour – and from that fusion there was created the most distinctive, remarkable and significant of all forms of human bondage.

Like so many important historical phenomena the origins of the European enslavement of Africans was accidental and haphazard. There had been, it is true, contact between the Europeans and Africans for centuries, primarily via the overland routes across the Sahara or along the Nile. Indeed Africans had found their way to the northern-most parts of Europe long before European maritime trade began to trespass on the coastline of black Africa.[2] Individual European voyages had also broken through the normal limitations on contemporary seafaring to reach the eastern Americas long before Columbus and his successors, but this does not detract from the stunning and revolutionary impact of the Iberian voyages in the fifteenth century. Portugal which had the important advantage of being a politically united kingdom, looked for a route round Africa partly to extend the crusade against the 'infidel' Turks and partly to seek whatever material rewards might lie in wait. Rumours about

7. The coast of West Africa showing the main slave-trading region in the late seventeenth century

Black Africa were confirmed and given specific detail by the fall to Portugal of the city of Ceuta in 1415. Most seductive of all was the evidence of African gold – Guinea gold. To be able to sail direct to West Africa would hence have the uniquely valuable and attractive qualities of combining crusading passion with economic reward. Armed with the powerful authorisation of Papal Bulls and urged on by the curiosity and enterprise of the royal court – particularly by Prince Henry the Navigator – the Portuguese embarked on that series of voyages which ultimately resulted in the European settlement and exploitation of parts of West Africa. Henry, whose coffers were empty, was seeking economic salvation from Guinea gold, but in the event his country's finances were to be enhanced by a quite unforeseen development – the slave trade.

The early slave trade consisted merely of raids on African settlements on the Saharan and then sub-Saharan coastline, and it is significant that those early raids were described by contemporaries as knightly and crusading deeds. Slowly, however, it became clear that peaceful trading for black Africans was more manageable – and profitable – than slave raiding. At first the Portuguese used their boats anchored off-shore as a base for their slaving activities, but about 1445 they built their first land-based slave 'factory' as a trading depot. It was the first of a string of such establishments which, over the coming centuries, were to dot the African coastline. As slaves and other African commodities began to filter back to Portugal, the commercial attractions of the region became manifest,

8. Portuguese slaving castle at Elmina on the Gold Coast, built in 1481

9 and 10. Two West African slaving forts, from eighteenth-century engravings

attracting ever more merchants and traders to venture into the risky
waters of the West African trade, much of which was devoted to the
capture and sale of the Africans.[3]

As the Portuguese cautiously threaded their way along the north-
west coastline they also discovered Madeira, the Azores, and the
Cape Verde islands which they promptly settled, an experience which
provided invaluable lessons of foreign settlement and plantation;
lessons which were to be of such value later in the Americas.
Equally, the practical results of these long-distance overseas
navigations were to prove important for subsequent voyages and
explorations across the Atlantic. Having established viable trading

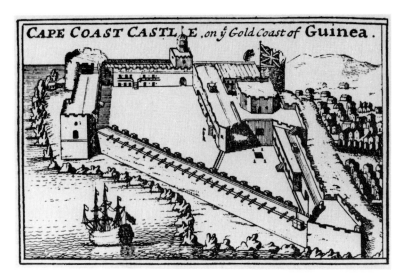

11. Cape Coast Castle, a slaving station

posts on the West African coastline, the Portuguese were able to
divert much of the gold which had previously crossed the desert in
Arab and Berber hands, into their own maritime accounts. Gold,
like slaves and other exotic commodities was shipped north to
Portugal, enhancing royal and mercantile wealth and expanding yet
further the growing European interest in West Africa. Portuguese
wealth was only the most obvious of a series of striking
consequences of this trade, but perhaps even more stunning were the
thousands of black slaves who began to appear in Portugal and her
possessions. Other Europeans, notably the Spaniards, had also
developed an interest in black slaves, with the result that by 1500
some 175,000 Africans had been shipped from Africa to Europe, the
Atlantic islands and Sao Tome.[4]

By that date the Portuguese and the Spaniards had extended their exploratory activities and were making initial probes on the western Atlantic and the Portuguese had even progressed into the Indian Ocean. Between 1500 and 1534 the Portuguese made numerous trading visits to Brazil, returning with local woods and animals. The threat of French intervention persuaded them to embark on permanent settlement. Land in Brazil was divided and allocated, with royal government operating through a governor-general in Bahia (1549). Alongside the early settlers, most of whom were rough and desperate men, lived the Jesuits whose task it was to convert the Indians. But as the settlements expanded and as they turned increasingly to the cultivation of sugar, it was soon apparent that there was simply not enough suitable local labour for that labour-intensive crop. Local Indians could not be recruited in sufficient numbers and would not, or could not, apply themselves to the difficult tasks demanded by the new system of cultivation. Even the enslavement of Indians – quite contrary to Portuguese law – failed to solve the problem and consequently from the mid-sixteenth century onwards there was a marked labour shortage in the Brazilian settlements. It took no great leap of the imagination to think that Africans might supply the necessary muscle power. After all the Portuguese were already using black slaves for similar work in the Atlantic islands and in Portugal itself. Sao Tome, for instance, had already been converted from an uninhabited island into a flourishing sugar producer – thanks to the use of African slaves. It seemed quite natural and logical to transplant this experience to Brazil. The only substantial difference was the necessity of making the Atlantic crossing.

Even here there were helpful precedents to follow since the Spaniards and others had already begun to ship Africans into perpetual bondage in the Americas. Blacks, for instance, had travelled with Columbus on his pioneering voyages, but the first effective slave cargo, of seventeen Africans, sailed to Hispaniola in 1505. Within a few years, regular supplies of African slaves began to arrive, to work the embryonic sugar plantations and mines of the Antilles. What determined and shaped the demand for black labour was, as in Brazil, the particular economy of the Spanish settlements in the Caribbean and Central America, with their labour-intensive activities and the inability or unsuitability of local Indians to undertake those tasks. Spanish settlers were dazzled by the success and prosperity of their new sugar settlements (so voracious had the new European demand for cane sugar become). But its cultivation was quite impossible without a large and expansive labour force and the necessary capital for the costly establishment of a sugar plantation. Backed by European capital, a system evolved of feeding more and more Africans into the buoyant sugar economy. As a result, the human face of the settlements was utterly transformed. So great was the importation of Africans that one Spanish commentator remarked, 'the land seems an effigy of Ethiopia itself'.[5]

Spanish settlers could never get enough Africans – at the right prices – largely because of an effective Portuguese monopoly on the African coast. But as the demands of the sugar settlements continued unsatisfied they began to attract the attention of a new species of merchants: the Atlantic slave traders. With a European base and contacts in West Africa, the slave traders began to ship growing numbers of Africans into bondage, in return for the produce, species and metals of the New World. Sometimes their ventures were legal; often they were quite illicit (in terms of the prevailing Iberian monopoly) but profits were good and the prospects of rich pickings proved more than enough to lure men of flair and enterprise. It was in this fashion that the English first became embroiled in the system which they did not institute, but which they were to perfect in years to come.

John Hawkins, a West Country merchant and sailor, had heard of the commercial needs of the West Indies on his trips to the Canaries. Among other things he learned that 'Negroes were very good merchandise in Hispaniola and that store of Negroes might easily be had upon the coast of Guinea'. Raising financial backing in London and his home West Country, he was able to sail in 1562 to Sierra Leone where he 'got into his possession, partly by the sworde, and partly by other meanes, to the number of 300 Negros at the least'. Sailing to the Spanish West Indies 'where he had peaceable traffique, and made vent of the whole of his Negros', Hawkins finally arrived home in September 1563 'with prosperous successe and much gaine to himselfe and the aforesaid adventurers'.[6]

Hawkins' success dangled the irresistible temptation before other enterprising men and it was quite clear that the monopoly agreement between Spain and Portugal which governed the old slave trade was no longer capable of satisfying the demand for slaves. What was needed was a much freer trade in slaves, and Hawkins' success gave great hope to other prospective interlopers.

By the early seventeenth century that monopoly was challenged by the rising power of the Dutch. The Portuguese bases in Africa and the firm plantation economies of Brazil (Pernambuco, Bahia and Rio) were severely shaken by the Dutch emergence. The Dutch raided Portuguese ports in West Africa, Brazil and even in Asia, and attacked Spanish settlements in South and Central America. At the heart of the struggle, which lasted until the mid-seventeenth century, lay the quest for free trade and commerce. The Dutch were keen to wrest from the Portuguese the sugar production of Brazil and the West African slave trade (and the Asian spice trade).[7] The peace which settled by the mid-seventeenth century left Portugal with her possessions in Angola, Bengal, Sao Tome and Principe, but the Dutch had secured the bases on the Gold Coast. In Brazil, after initial successes, the Dutch were driven out but not to be utterly denied access to the wealth promoted by sugar, they fled from Pernambuco, taking the expertise, finance and experience of planting to Guiana and, later, to Barbados. In exactly these years the British began settlements of their own in the Caribbean and North America and they, like the Dutch, adopted the patterns already established in the past 150 years by their Iberian rivals and settled in plantations. Spanish military and mercantile power was broken and the Caribbean fell to the north Europeans. Similarly, the Portuguese monopoly in slave trading had effectively ended and the way was now open for newcomers. With their political and economic stars in the ascendancy, it was natural that the British and the Dutch would profit from the collapse of Iberian power, and it was inevitable that they would feud over the global spoils. When in 1645 George Downing wrote of Barbados, he remarked:

> You will see a flourishing Island, many able men, I believe they have bought this year no lesse than a thousand Negroes, and the more they buie the better able they are to buye, for in a yeare and a halfe they will earn (with God's blessing) as much as they cost . . .[8]

But behind this beguilingly simple formula there lay a complex social and economic formulation.

In the early seventeenth century the British and other northern Europeans gradually established themselves on a number of Caribbean islands, pushing aside the enfeebled Spaniards (and indigenous peoples) and slowly securing a viable economy in the midst of a luxuriant natural habitat. It was, however, a difficult environment to work in; clearing the bush and laying the basis of a viable agriculture was consuming of manpower and capital. Of course the impetus to colonisation was far distant from the region itself and had first emerged under Elizabeth I. But it was not until the reign of James I that Englishmen made significant progress in securing a number of footholds in the New World. There were, naturally, failures and consequent human disasters but gradually trial and error, with the correct additives of careful planning and good fortune, ensured the survival of some of the settlements. Many of the early Stuart adventurers sought gold, making tentative and ill-fated settlements in Guiana, Trinidad and St Lucia, led most notably by Sir Walter Raleigh. Better luck was had by those Englishmen who settled in the Lesser Antilles. St Kitts (Christopher) was settled in

12. An Amerindian taken into slavery after the war between Indians and settlers in South Carolina, 1680

1624 and its land turned to tobacco production: a crop which was easily grown and which found an expanding market thanks to the Englishman's new-found smoking habits. Charles I, anxious to promote other American settlements, gave patents to authorise the settlement of Nevis, Barbados and Montserrat. By the time Barbados was founded in 1627, about sixty black slaves had already been introduced to the tobacco culture of St Kitts. In Barbados, however, the first enslaved labourers were Amerindians and in both islands the pioneering labour force was set to the task of burning the bush-forest and clearing the land for planting. For the desperate – or adventurous – these islands beckoned as an opportunity to escape from the miseries of Britain. But these early years were difficult, and were riven by personal rivalries and consequent economic dislocation, quite apart from the privations which seemed to be the natural lot of all pioneering settlers – and the dislocation caused by Indian and Spanish attacks.

Labour was obviously in short supply in the Caribbean settlements although in the early years the work of establishing the rudiments of agriculture was not as labour intensive as was to become the case later. In 1640 sugar planting was introduced into Barbados, primarily at Dutch instigation and within a very short time sugar was the main crop of the island – and subsequently of the whole Caribbean. Unlike earlier products, however, sugar needed labourers in numbers and intensity which existing supplies were quite incapable of satisfying. The indentured white servants, imported from Ireland, Scotland and England, were not numerous enough, and could not be readily and swiftly replaced for efficient management of the new sugar plantations. Africans, on the other hand, seemed to fit the bill perfectly and, furthermore, had already been used extensively as slaves by the Spaniards and Portuguese in their own colonial settlements. Sugar rapidly established itself as *the* powerful economic force which lured the slave cargoes across the Atlantic in growing numbers. In the early 1640s there were, in Barbados, only 6400 slaves (and 2500 whites); by 1650 there were some 20,000 slaves. By 1680 there were about 37,000 slaves but only 17,000 whites, and as the numbers of African slaves increased the size of the sugar plantations expanded, gobbling up ever more land and putting an end to the initial small holdings.[9] Much the same pattern unfolded in Jamaica which was taken by the British from the Spanish in 1655. There the establishment of sugar rapidly transformed the island into a black society. In 1670 there were some 7000 slaves (and whites); by 1690 the Jamaican slaves outnumbered the whites by four to one. By 1700 Jamaica was home to 45,000 slaves – and had become the world's biggest sugar producer. Eighty years later in 1780 there were some 200,000 slaves on the island.[10] Thus in Barbados, Jamaica and elsewhere the early European settlements had been revolutionised by sugar production and had in the process been utterly transformed into black slave societies. And the same pattern (though with variations) was evident throughout the region. By 1700, for instance, the French had imported about 16,000 slaves into Martinique and 20,000 into St Domingue; by the mid-eighteenth century the black population of the latter stood at about a half million. While clearly not all these slaves worked in sugar, it is nonetheless the case that it was the ramifications of sugar cultivation which established the rapid growth in the slave trade across the Atlantic and the demographic revolution in the Caribbean. As a result the plantation colonies became unalterably black – and enslaved.

If the Caribbean and South America had long been attractive areas for European settlement, in time the vast spaces of North America proved no less seductive. Between 1600–1700 the Europeans transformed the eastern coastal region, some 360,000 square miles, stretching from the present-day Maine to Georgia. By 1700, the indigenous peoples had been pushed back from the coast and their former lands devoured by the half million Europeans (mainly British and Dutch). By then there were between 10–20,000 enslaved blacks in the colonies. All but the Africans were lured to North America by expectations of a better life or freedom from European oppression. In the early stages and like their counterparts in the Caribbean, the settlers' aspirations withered in the appallingly harsh conditions of pioneering life. The farm settlements in Virginia were narrowly secured after a series of disasters, and the land was turned to self-sufficiency and manageable crops (notably tobacco). Small plantations helped gradually to spread the area of cultivable land, but most of the labour on that land was undertaken by the land-owners and their indentured servants shipped out from Britain. The human cost, thanks to the ravages of disease, hunger and Indian wars, was appalling. But the pattern of settlement and development was well established.

Throughout the northern colonies (and again as in the Caribbean) labour was at a premium. Although some 1500 indentured servants arrived in Virginia annually throughout much of the seventeenth century, these numbers were rarely sufficient and to make matters worse many indentured servants expected to become independent land-owners when they had served their time.

Black slaves were used from an early date but not in any significant numbers. Black 'servants' had been deposited in Virginia in 1619 by a Dutch vessel and although Virginian law did not formally recognise slavery until 1661, in economic practice in the colony the black was soon relegated to a level of inferiority within the local social structure.[11] By 1650 there were only 150 blacks in

Virginia – and not all were slaves – but by 1680 this had risen to 3000. At the turn of the century there were perhaps 10,000 blacks in the colony (though by that date in Jamaica there were 45,000). As the number of Virginian blacks increased they became more important to the local economy, though this is in many respects to invert the natural formula since they were imported primarily to fill a labour need. Yet the most significant transition was not simply their growth in absolute numbers but the evolution in Virginia of an institution which was common throughout the British Caribbean and South America: black chattel slavery.

The limitations on the freedom of white indentured servants (which in many cases had simply not been enforceable) became less striking with the rise of black slavery. As white workers became freer, the blacks became more and more enslaved. The end result of these two related through divergent patterns was the loosening of the legal and economic shackles of the white workers and their tightening over the black. By the end of the seventeenth century slavery was a well-established institution in the North American colonies, in law and in practice, though it was nothing like as important as it was in other parts of the Americas. Henceforth and until black emancipation in the nineteenth century, the black American slave was not merely the lowest type of servant but became a piece of property, a chattel and a thing 'to be bought and sold, a status applicable only and necessarily to blacks and to their descendants to the ultimate degree'.[12] In 1705 a young Virginian, Robert Beverley, aptly described the distinctions now demarcating the servants from the slaves. 'Slaves are the negroes and their posterity, following the condition of the mother . . . . They are called slave in respect of the time of their servitude because it is for life. Servants are those which serve only for a few years, according to the time of their indenture, or the custom of their country.'[13]

A number of the northern colonies established their own slave codes (or laws) to deal with the complex difficulties created by the evolution of an enslaved black population. These laws, in conjunction with the economic development of bondage itself, were to form the basis for the American experience of slavery for the best part of two centuries – years which witnessed the massive geographic expansion of the American polity, the economic revolution (particularly of cotton) and the demographic explosion in the slave communities. From the small-scale, haphazard and economically insignificant origins of American bondage, there was to blossom a major institution with incalculable human consequences which were to plague and to trouble the subsequent history of the American republic. As the colonies expanded westward and to the south, black slaves followed the trail of the expanding American empire, undertaking the burdens of arduous pioneering work and helping to render the alien land cultivable and profitable.

The emergence of slavery in the northern colonies was hardly surprising since some of the colonies had close ties with the Caribbean slave islands. Indeed the ties between the Caribbean and the North Americans were often extremely important. Some northern colonies were themselves able to grow the tropical produce, and with that in mind 'seasoned' slaves were shipped north from the Caribbean to the mainland. In South Carolina (a Restoration settlement) where rice became a staple crop, the conditions endured by local slaves were harsh, and their role was confirmed by local laws which were modelled on the severe slave codes of Barbados.[14] The expansion of planting economy – tobacco in Virginia, rice in Carolina – created demands for labour which simply could not be met by the inflow of indentured whites, but which might apparently more easily be satisfied by the purchase of black slaves. To many contemporaries it seemed obvious that slaves were cheaper than indentured labourers (though now it seems that the economic formula was both more complex and much less clear). This preference soon found a reflection in slave importations. Between 1700–20 some 20,000 slaves entered British North America; in the next twenty years a further 50,000 arrived. Moreover the demographic picture was much starker in particular regions. The blacks formed 40 per cent of Virginia's population in the 1730s; in South Carolina by 1720 they outnumbered the whites by two to one. In Jamaica at the same time they overwhelmed the local whites by more than six to one.[15] But the American slave owners, unlike their Caribbean counterparts, rarely held more than a handful of slaves, a fact which was to have major repercussions for slave history.

By 1700 the European conquerors and settlers of the New World had securely established their hold over enormous expanses of the Americas. The North and South American interiors were to provide unimagined scope for expansion and exploitation over the next two centuries. But the political and economic systems and the legal practices firmly entrenched by that date in the settled Americas were to prove remarkably resilient and adaptable in accommodating later changes. Where slavery had been introduced into the tropical colonies, it was to remain a fundamental and unchallenged institution for many years to come. Moreover, black slavery 'spilled over' into regions which lacked the basic economic need for cheap and easily replaceable labour. Thus it was to be found in New York, Rhode Island, New England – and even in England itself. The discoveries of the wider world, their economic exploitation by expansive European societies and the harnessing of African labour to tap the economic potential of the Americas, all in complex conjunction with each other, established not merely European societies in the New World, but began to populate parts of the Americas with the peoples of Africa.

The European settlements stemmed initially from decisions, however painful or complex, to emigrate. The Africans, however, made no such decision, but were driven into a lifetime's bondage and were then obliged to bequeath their status to their descendants. The growing and apparently insatiable demand for black labour created not merely an international trade – the trans-Atlantic slave trade – of enormous proportions, but set in train the African diaspora, a process which was to reshape the demographic face of the western world.

4. The African Diaspora

The movement of African people from their homelands to the far reaches of the Atlantic empires was to be, in retrospect, the most significant and large-scale enforced movement of peoples in the premodern world. The compulsory emigration of black Africans took place over a period of many centuries. If we include the trans-Saharan shipment of Africans to the Mediterranean which became significant in the ninth century, then we are dealing with a migration which spanned 1000 years. It was, however, in the years of European ascendancy, from the fifteenth century to the nineteenth, that this African diaspora reached staggeringly high levels; draining certain African societies of their healthy and largely young labour force and in the process transforming the economics and demographic face of the New World settlements. Naturally enough from such complex and confused historical upheavals it is enormously difficult to assess the numbers of people involved and in fact this topic has become a major academic growth industry. The numbers of Africans forced to leave their homelands is still disputed and various scholars have calculated the total to be anything from ten to twenty-five million. The standard authority, Philip Curtin, convincingly argues that somewhere in the region of ten million Africans landed in the Americas, but there were also to be counted in their millions many more who did not survive capture, upheaval and transportation.[1] Other historians have argued that these figures are too low. It has been claimed, for instance, that some ten millions were taken to the Mediterranean, the Red Sea and the Indian Ocean and by adding these figures together it has been calculated that twenty-five million Africans were wrenched from their homes in the millenium from the ninth century onwards.[2]

Whichever figure we find most convincing, they represent an unparalled degree of human misery and social dislocation. The African slave trade was not, however, a uniform trade or population movement, but had remarkable diversity and changes both across time and from place to place. In large measure the drain of black population was a direct response to the demand outside Africa for black labour. In the early years of the trans-Sahara trade for instance the taste for black domestic slaves emanated from the homes of prosperous Mediterranean people who sought in their black domestics not merely household labour but, equally important, social cudos and an enhancement of their own social status. Black slaves were luxury items to adorn the homes and social standing of the wealthy. Often, however, Africans had more economically-useful roles, serving as soldiers in the Mediterranean and as agricultural workers in some of the economic transformations apparent in that region in the early Middle Ages. Africans and their descendants formed a large servile rural labour force in Iraq, Bahrein and along the north African coast – and all this long before the Europeans had embarked on their major voyages of discovery and overseas settlement. Well before Europeans began to recruit African slaves, blacks in their thousands had fallen prey to the efficient and extensive overland slave trading systems of the Arabs and Berbers.

The existence of this overland trade is important not merely in its own terms but also in relation to the subsequent development of the Atlantic slave trade. When the early European voyages first put ashore in West Africa they came into contact with societies which already had experience of slaving. To admit the revolutionary and transforming impact of the European demand for slaves from the 15th century onwards is not to claim that black slavery was invented by the white traders. It clearly was not – even though they elevated it and perfected it to a level and intensity unimaginable in the pre-colonial world. Two points need to be made in this respect. The overland slave trade, with the consequent demand for servile labour, long pre-dates the European involvement in black slavery and secondly there clearly existed, in a host of African societies groups of people who occupied servile status. Of course it might be argued that such servility does not amount to slavery *tout court*. Yet it seems reasonable to argue that such servile status was, under certain conditions, easily transmuted into chattel slavery. And this was particularly the case under external pressure and the demand for cheap, pliant enslaved people. Whether at the behest of the overland or later the Atlantic slave traders, Africans were sold or bartered, *as things*. Naturally enough the nature of the African in a servile status varied enormously, between the different social structures, regions and time.[3] But it was the *outside* pressures and demands for labour which proved crucial in the development of chattel slavery from its chrysalis as African servitude.

Despite recent important revisionary work it seems clear that when Europeans first landed in West Africa they were faced with a number of societies which possessed slaves – though not always a separate *class* of slaves.[4] Thus the Europeans were able to tap and then to transform existing forms of servitude and convert them to their own ends. Whatever distinctive form African bondage had taken, it was the outside demand for black labour, notably from the Americas which was to give it those characteristics which were endured by the greatest number of people and hence are best remembered. Yet it is important to remember that the very fact that slavery in the Americas, notably plantation slavery, *is* so well known (though often in caricatured form) has distorted our image – and even the historical questions we ask – of African servile labour before the arrival of the Europeans. There is a seductive temptation to look backwards from mature American slavery and to imagine that African servitude was the same. It was not.

The Europeans did not, then, initiate black servitude but rather inherited it, though it is also true that they perfected a new form of slavery and slowly imposed it on unprecedented numbers of people and large tracts of the newly conquered Americas. In this process their first task was simply to acquire the slaves. Throughout the subsequent history of black slavery the source of African slaves was a bitterly disputed issue which hinged upon arguments of whether the European demand for slaves was the cause and stimulus for the enslavement and relegation of Africans to the level of property. It seems fairly clear that Africans were sold into slavery for a number of reasons: for crimes, for instance, though it is impossible to tell how common this was. The overwhelming bulk of slaves were

13. Imaginary reconstruction of bartering slaves between Europeans and Africans

acquired by warfare (as had been the pattern in the classical world) or by raids. Some indication of this pattern is the fact that some of the main commodities used by Europeans in bartering for slaves were firearms and weapons – invaluable of course in the enslavement process. The evidence for African enslavement is elusive and fragmentary, and this is particularly the case from the African viewpoint. But in 1789 a former slave, Olaudah Equiano,

14. Olaudah Equiano, a former slave, who became a prominent spokesman of the English black community in the 1780s and 1790s

published an invaluable account of his own enslavement more than forty years before.

> One day, when all our people were gone out to their work as usual and only I and my dear sister were left to mind the house, two men and a woman got over our walls, and in a moment seized us both, and without giving us time to cry out to make resistance they stopped our mouths and ran off with us into the nearest woods.

There followed a long and difficult journey lasting for months, in which Equiano passed through a series of African societies before arriving on the Atlantic coast and coming face to face with European slave traders.

> I was immediately handled and tossed up to see if I were sound by some of the crew, and I was now persuaded that I had gotten into a world of bad spirits and that they were going to kill me. Their complexions too differing so much from ours, that their long hair and the language they spoke . . . united to confirm me in this belief.[5]

Equiano's account is very instructive (even when allowance is made for its obvious shortcomings). Long before meeting the European traders, he had been enslaved by other Africans and passed along a complex African trading nexus which deposited him and countless others at the white man's disposal on the coast. Of course it could be countered, would this have been possible without the pull of the European coastal trading presence and the white demand for African slaves? This historical conundrum is in effect unanswerable. But what is undeniable is that by the time European settlements in the New World had become addicted to slave labour, the consequent slave trade undoubtedly dictated the motive, pace and extent of slave trading among the Africans far into the African interior.

When in the later eighteenth and early nineteenth centuries the slave traders and owners came under attack, they frequently asserted that slavery was no less than salvation for the enslaved Africans, who would, as prisoners of war, have been slaughtered (they claimed) had there been no slave trade. Despite the stridency and frequency of this argument it was flawed by retrospection, and of course it was a tactical rather than a historical case. Furthermore it could be legitimately countered that, as the slave trade grew in size and sophistication many such African conflicts were directly stimulated by the needs of the slave trade itself. Victorious tribes or groups would know that their captives could provide a lucrative

15. Slavery in the Sudan in the late nineteenth century

16. A slave coffle

commodity to be fed into the voracious jaws of the slaving machine. Yet this, like many other explanations or justifications for the African involvement in slave trading, is largely hypothetical and rests on debatable evidence. It is furthermore pointless to seek a single, seminal cause of African slaving, apart from the growing economic demand for cheap and pliant labour in the Americas. Once that demand had been established, however, its consequences for sub-Saharan Africa were far-reaching and fundamental.

The most obvious impact was the drain of population. The enforced movement of so many millions of Africans is naturally *the* most striking and indelible fact of the trans-Atlantic trade. Not only did it populate large regions of the New World and, at a more recent date, parts of Europe itself, with an alien and alienated black population but it removed from African societies valuable labour. Healthy young Africans were prized above all others (Equiano for instance was only twelve when enslaved) – the very people often most important in a number of agricultural societies. It is difficult to assess the manifold and perhaps conflicting effects which this drain of population had upon Africa. Some states flourished – briefly – on the proceeds of slaving. On the other hand there were political conflicts, upheavals and social tensions inevitably created by the slave trade. Similarly, the infiltration of firearms had a damaging and destabilising effect on African life. The ramifications of the slave trade were remarkably complex. At its most obvious, because of the continuing loss of people, African societies failed to develop as they might, although we need not accept the more general proposition recently advanced by Walter Rodney that Europe underdeveloped Africa.[6] Although it is true that slave trading was only *one* aspect of a complex European trading presence, it seems indisputable that the European demand for African slaves had a series of baneful and even catastrophic effects on African societies.

The African diaspora was not a uniform nor a consistent phenomenon either in time or place. It affected different African societies differently and some indication of this can be seen in the chronological development of the Atlantic slave trade. The first region to develop slave-trading contacts was that first probed by the Europeans – Senegambia. Indeed up to 1600 something like one-third of all exported slaves came from this region – increasingly from the distant interior.[7] Further south on the Upper Guinea and Sierra Leone coasts, the Portuguese established their important slaving presence in the course of the fifteenth and sixteenth centuries and it was to this region that the British were lured once they heard of its profitability. But the overall slave-trading value of this region declined in the seventeenth century (though there were to be a number of minor revivals generally associated with upheavals in the interior).

Further to the south and east, the region known as the Windward Coast was traditionally unrewarding for slave traders. This was partly due to geographical and physical factors. It was, quite simply, difficult to find good anchorage or port facilities, and these physical disadvantages inhibited an effective European slave-trading presence. Consequently local slaves, or those from the interior, tended to be sold through neighbouring regions and outlets. Further east still lay the Gold Coast, its name alone giving the clue to its prime economic importance to the predatory Europeans. To this day the great forts and castles which dot the coastline are a reminder of European fears and insecurities in defending their gold – not against the Africans but against other Europeans. From the mid-seventeenth century onwards slaves became increasingly important exports from this region and by the end of that century perhaps three-quarters of the region's export-values derived from slaves and not from gold: an obvious reflection of the parallel expansion of new lands in the Americas.[8]

Not all African states succumbed to the blandishments of the slavers. Some, powerful and assertive when the Europeans arrived (Benin, for instance), refused to involve themselves in any significant way. Under the right conditions, 'one option open to a major African state was simply not to participate in the slave trade'.[9] In fact such conscious refusal was unusual; more common was the submission or co-operation of African societies to the blandishments or threats of the Europeans. The Congo and Angola regions provide perhaps the most vivid examples of the European slaving presence. There, powerful African kingdoms and cultures rose and fell, undermined directly or indirectly by the corrosive European demand for African slaves. Whatever the local African peculiarities, there slowly evolved an international trade in people; a diaspora of Africans which flung its victims to the far reaches of European trade and settlement.

Thus, although it is tempting to speak of European slave trading in Africa in generalised terms, it is crucial to bear in mind the major differences in slaving experience between the different regions of West Africa. Equally it is important to stress that, with time and the growing demand for African slaves the internal African slaving networks became more elaborate and extensive, stretching far into what Europeans would have regarded as the 'darkest' of interiors. Many slaves, like Equiano who had never even heard of the existence of white people, were ultimately delivered to the white traders on the coast.

The engine behind the Atlantic slave trade was European settlement and economic change in the western Atlantic. When Europe 'discovered' America there were an estimated 100 million indigenous Indians there; within a century there remained only 10 millions.[10] Although there were perhaps 800,000 white colonists scattered throughout the region in the mid-seventeenth century they could in no way fill the labour vacuum created by the catastrophical collapse of the native populations – even if they wished to. Europeans were already familiar with those African slaves imported into Europe before 1500. Now the Americas called out for them in menial capacity and servile status. Gradually the Africans and their descendants began to outnumber the initial small bands of white settlers throughout the hemisphere. In the Spanish settlements, for instance, Africans played a crucial role in the initial military and economic settlements and by 1650 there were perhaps one-third of a million black slaves and about 135,000 mulattos scattered throughout Spanish America.[11]

The northern Europeans fared worse as far as local labour was concerned, for the indigenous Indians died out or were reduced to small handfuls. Yet the new economic developments, particularly the sugar plantations, were labour intensive and from an early date established a voracious appetite for human beasts of burden. Sugar cultivation spread from north-eastern Brazil to the new settlements of the Caribbean and as each island or region fell to the economic seductions of sugar, it was progressively converted into a black society. By the end of the eighteenth century the British and French islands in the Caribbean were home to more than one million slaves.[12]

The white settlements in North America were quite different from those in the Caribbean but, as we have seen, where tropical crops were developed, Africans were inexorably drawn into the colony. By the end of the eighteenth century some three-quarters of a million Africans or their descendants lived in the region. Yet it was the cotton revolution of the early nineteenth century which transformed American slavery. The black population of the USA – some 2,800,000 in 1840 – followed the geographic drift away from the old slave states. What was remarkable, and distinctive, about US slavery was its demographic buoyancy. Unlike the tropical colonies in the Caribbean and South America, the USA soon lost its need for importations of African slaves for the simple reason that the local slave population bred and thrived. Expanding slave colonies (and later states) could always find fresh supplies of black labour locally; Brazil, Cuba and Jamaica on the other hand were traditionally forced to look to Africa to replenish their supplies of slaves. The reasons for these different patterns of reproduction are extremely complex and relate to the sex ratio among slaves, their age structure and to the wider geophysical environment in which slave work (and life) was conducted. Stated crudely, however, it seems likely that the nature of US slave work by the early nineteenth century, that is cotton, and the physical habitat in which it thrived, were less arduous and less disruptive both socially and physically than work on a sugar plantation or in mines. Another indication of the more benign nature of US slavery is to be seen in the incidence of open resistance which, by any criterion was remarkably less frequent, violent, successful or widespread compared with slave revolts in the Caribbean or South America. This is not to suggest that US slaves were docile, but rather that their lot was quite different from that of slaves in other regions; and their responses were consequently different.[13]

In time economic fluctuations in the slave-holding countries imposed variations on the pace of African transportation. African importations were, for instance, stimulated by the economic revival of Spanish America – in Central America and the Caribbean – with a result that some two million slaves had been imported into those possessions by about 1800. Much the same pattern took place in Brazil in the eighteenth century, but there the economic motive was the development of the slave-worked mines of the interior. In the nineteenth century, however, it was the economic transformation of Cuba and Brazil which gave Atlantic slave trading a new lease of life. The destruction of slave society in Haiti in the 1790s made available sugar expertise and also created a demand for the produce formerly grown in Haiti. Cuba benefited from both these factors and rapidly established itself as the region's major sugar producer with a consequent upsurge in its black slave population. By the end of the nineteenth century there were more than half a million Africans and their descendants on the island.[14] A similar boom in Brazil – for coffee – drew further cargoes of Africans across the Atlantic and by 1872 there was an African-based population of 5,700,000 living in Brazil.[15] Thus the slave ships continued to sail to Brazil and Cuba until the mid-nineteenth century, depositing in those burgeoning economies unprecedented numbers of Africans.

The millions of Africans who crossed the Atlantic – from such diverse regions and destined for the full range of praedial life throughout the Americas – shared the common experience and the horrors of the Middle Passage. While historians have been able to reconstruct the details of the Atlantic crossings – the size of ships, of slave cargoes, mortality rates, slaves' illnesses and their commercial values – it seems practically impossible to convey the appalling experiences of the slaves crossing the Atlantic.

The Atlantic slave trade emerged from its *ad hoc* beginnings into a major source of international trade, an issue in international diplomacy and warfare, and a direct stimulus to the development of a wide range of European economic activity. Cities grew to prominence in large measure because of their involvement in slaving, with the inevitable stimulus to their economic hinterland and the ancillary development of finance, banking and insurance. In the early days of the trade, however, it was loosely organised; a small group of friends and associates (like the first Hawkins venture) investing capital in a speculative maritime enterprise whose main commodity was humans rather than inanimate items of trade. This private enterprise soon gave way to state monopolies (itself an indication of the importance which European nations came to attach to the slave trade) but these slave-trading monopolies soon proved inadequate to feed the colonial appetite for slaves. The slave trade reached its apogee not through monopoly trading, but by virtue of a largely free trade system which lured investors, traders, sailors and merchants into the attractive – though often fatal and unprofitable – trans-Atlantic trade.

17. Branding slaves in Africa, after Briand

In time the commercial and organisational structure of the slave trade became increasingly complex. But such organisational and commercial details were of no interest to the victims; the millions of Africans who found themselves herded and shackled into the pestilential holds of the slave ships. In time there developed 'custom-built' slave ships, designed and planned for maximum efficiency in the loading of human beings. And it is from the heyday of slave trading in the eighteenth and nineteenth centuries that the best-remembered (if appalling) images survive; of packed holds and of Africans crammed onto shelves and racks amidst scenes of unimaginable wretchedness.

The loading of ships in West Africa varied enormously. In places, where the coast afforded no natural harbour or anchorage, the European vessels took on their human cargoes at sea, at bases on off-shore islands or from smaller, shallow-draft boats and tenders. Elsewhere the slaves were herded in large groups into 'factories' to be inspected or bartered – and often branded.[16] From the factories, the slaves were

> sold in open Market on shore, and examined by us in like manner, as our Brother Trade do Beasts in Smithfield; the Countenance, and Stature, a good Set of Teeth, Pliancy in their Limbs, and Joints, and being free of Venereal Taint . . . .[17]

At other places trading took place in tents on beaches, after which skilled African canoeists manoeuvred small coffles of slaves from the beach to anchored slaving ships. As with many other areas of trade, much depended on luck, notably whether there would be enough healthy slaves available. Much, too, depended on the skill and experience of the slave master and his 'surgeon' in spotting ailments. Throughout, however, the virtues of good management and shrewd dealings could be overwhelmed by the accidents of fate. One diseased slave could spread fatal havoc among the human cargo and crew. Moreover, it was appreciated that the longer a ship tarried on the African coast, the more likely it was that the whites too would fall victim to the region's notorious diseases. Whites resident on the coasts tended not to survive long but died quickly and in horrifying numbers. So too did the crews of the slave ships. Indeed the white crews of these ships suffered a mortality rate which was proportionately higher than that for the slaves.

Often a slaver would have to wait a considerable time before acquiring an adequate black cargo and often had to visit various spots on the coast, buying a group here and a handful there. It seems to have been uncommon for a slaver to be able to take on board a

18. A slave market in Zanzibar

19. Haggling for slaves

20. An embarkation canoe transporting slaves to the slave ship

21. A slaver taking in negroes, 1844

full cargo. Once at sea and heading west for the Americas, ill-fortune could upset the best-planned and prepared of slave voyages. The most unpredictable factor was the weather. A stormy crossing would tax the crew to the limits (and slavers were normally understaffed) leaving little time to feed the slaves, tend the sick, remove the corpses (which, of course, remained shackled to the living) or to cleanse the fouled holds. Amidst these scenes of repulsive horror the African slaves might remain for days on end, untended, unfed and unclean; chained together, the living and the dead. As a slaver battled through an Atlantic storm, the scenes in the slave holds were of pestilential horror. Even in less taxing conditions the dangers were ever present. A contagious slave could decimate

22. Loading slaves in 1861

cargo and crew. In the words of one slave captain, 'What the small-pox spar'd, the flux swept off to our great regret'.[18] Again, Equiano's account is invaluable:

> The closeness of the place and the heat of the climate, added to the number in the ship, which was so crowded that each had scarcely room to turn himself, almost suffocating us. This produced copious persperations, so that the air soon became unfit for respiration from a variety of loathesome smells, and brought on a sickness among the slaves, of which many died.[19]

Disease was not the only danger to the whites. As soon as slaves were brought on board, the crew had to be perpetually vigilant against violence and revolt or suicide. On Equiano's ship, 'two of my wearied countrymen who were chained together . . . preferred death to such a life of misery, somehow made through the nettings and jumped into the sea'.[20] Perhaps even more alarming was the perpetual threat of revolt – easily imagined (if not so easily executed) when slaves found themselves confronted by such small groups of whites (who were, however, well armed). Armed guards, guns

23. A slave revolt on board ship

trained on the holds, slaves released for exercise in small batches, a regime of feeding and inspection which would be familiar in many modern prisons, all provide testimony to the perennial nightmare of shipboard revolt or violence. Generally slave revolts were suppressed, often even nipped in the bud, but there are numerous examples of major and successful slave revolts. Ten slavers from Nantes alone in the eighteenth century were completely overwhelmed by slave revolts.[21] John Newton, later to be an influential figure in the campaign against the slave trade, recorded how, when he was a slave ship captain, he had snuffed out a threatened slave revolt on his ship in 1752:

> By the favour of Divine Providence made a timely discovery today that the slaves were forming a plot for an insurrection. Surprised two of them attempting to get off their irons, and upon further search in their rooms, upon the information of 3 of the boys, found some knives, stones, shot, etc. . . . and a cold chisel. . . . Put the boys in irons and slightly in the thumbscrews to urge them to a full confession. . . .

A day later:

> in the morning examined the men slaves and punished 4 of them in collars.[22]

What carried off more slaves than revolt or suicide was disease and illness, not surprisingly perhaps when we consider that many if not most had walked for months before getting to the slave coast. Yet slave mortality was unpredictable and could vary from nought to utter devastation. In fact although the average slave mortality was high, this was largely because a minority of ships suffered catastrophic loss of life. But the great bulk lost relatively few slaves,[23] and as the slave trade developed, slave mortality fell, though the reasons remain unclear and are disputed. By the last years of the eighteenth century the mortality on British slavers had fallen below 5 per cent, though it seems to have remained at about 10 per cent among other European slave traders.[24] By that time there was, for instance, a growing awareness of health problems, an increased African immunity to particular ailments and a notable decline in epidemic diseases (the latter factor a crucial element in the population growth in contemporary Europe). Whatever the cause it seems to have been unrelated to 'packing' of slaves, for research has shown no real correlation between the degree of 'packing' and the incidence of slave mortality. It is true that the slave ships got bigger (though still only 200 tons on average by 1800)[25] and bigger ships tended to carry fewer slaves proportionate to their tonnage.

The one factor above all others which helps to explain the mortality rates is the time taken to cross the Atlantic; the longer the voyage the heavier the loss of slave life tended to be.[26] Dysentery – the bloody flux – was the most persistent of killers on the boats and the longer the journey the more likely the spread of pollution via food and water supplies.[27] And this was the case *irrespective* of the actions of the captain and crews. Even the most benign and considerate of regimes could do little to fend off such fatal attacks for the simple reason that the wider disease and health environment was generally beyond contemporary understanding or ability to alter.

While it is natural today to think of the traders as cruel men, they had every reason to take care of their valuable black cargoes. The more slaves they landed in a healthy condition, the more profitable the voyage. On the whole they tried to save their slaves – though not for reasons of tender humanity. There developed well-known procedures for cleansing and fumigating the ships and for giving the slaves a regular diet of food and water. It was well known among slavers that a successful (that is, profitable) voyage depended among other things upon 'the wholesome Victualling, and Management of Slaves on Board'.[28] By 1789 evidence was given to Parliament of the ideal daily routines on board a slave ship. Weather permitting, slaves were brought out daily, in batches to be 'rubbed down' and tended.

> The Surgeon, or his Mate, also generally attends to wash their Mouths with Vinegar or Lime Juice, in order to prevent Scurvy. After they are upon Deck, Water is handed to them to wash their Hands and Faces. They are then formed into Messes, consisting of Ten to each Mess, and a warm Mess is provided for them, alternatively of their own Country Food, and of the Pulse carried from Europe for that Purpose, to which Stock Fish, Palm Oil, Pepper, etc are added; after that, Water is handed them to drink.[29]

Needless to say this was the view from the slave traders' vantage point and it seems likely that in reality, life on the slave ship was quite different. But even if this scene were true to life, it would have been utterly disrupted by bad weather.

24. Slaves being forced to dance

Slaves were in greatest demand in the tropical colonies in the months January–June, that is the tropical harvest period. To cross the Atlantic took three or four months, depending not merely on weather conditions, but equally upon the points of departure and landfall. Because of prevailing winds and currents it was sometimes common for the shorter voyages to take longer than a more distant crossing. But whatever the details of the crossing the slavers had fairly precise knowledge and forewarning about how long their voyage would take and they could provision their vessel accordingly. It was also possible that such calculations could go disastrously wrong – with dire results for the slaves. In 1781 the British slave ship the *Zong*, unexpectedly delayed at sea and in danger of running short of supplies, simply dumped 132 slaves overboard in order to save the healthier slaves and on the understanding that such an action would be covered by the ship's insurance (not the case had the wretched slaves merely died).[30]

25. The British slave trade was abolished in 1807. Thereafter, slave traders sometimes threw slaves overboard to avoid being caught by Royal Navy patrols

This particular outrage became a *cause célèbre*, yet how many other similar incidents went unrecorded and unlamented? So far, it may be felt, the picture described here has been too charitable towards the slavers and does not fully underline the inhumanities endemic in the slave trade. It is true that the slave trade was an exercise in cruelty and inhumanity to a degree scarcely imaginable to modern readers. But there were also a myriad of injuries and pains endured by slaves on an individual basis. Slaves were sorted into groups, men and boys separate from the women and children (although many, if not most, had already been torn from their relatives and loved ones when enslaved). Women were exposed to the sexual assaults of the crew though some captains tried to prevent such incidents. But sadistic sailors (and we need to recall the unattractiveness of the job), conniving or malicious officers could and did compound the slaves' general miseries by acts of savage wickedness. Flogging of slaves, sexual abuse, starving the victims, all these were well known if not necessarily typical. One vicious captain flogged to death a slave child of nine months.[31] But for every recorded incident of this kind it is important to stress that the greatest cruelty of all was the slave trade itself; the institutionalisation of shipping millions of Africans into the Americas and reducing them in law, practice and in the eyes of the dominant whites to the level of beasts and property. It seems perfectly comprehensible that many when given the chance would do what one slave did on board an English slave ship in 1675–6: 'April Monday 17th . . . a stout man slave leaped overboard and drowned himself.'[32]

The horrors of the middle passage for the slaves are in no way minimised by pointing out that their captors, and often their tormentors, died and suffered too in greater proportion than the slaves themselves. In the 1780s and 1790s, for instance, 21.6 per cent of the crews of 350 slavers from Bristol and Liverpool died.[33] But the very great majority of deaths among the crews occurred when the slave ships were anchored off the African coast awaiting their cargoes.[34] Indeed it was this high white mortality rate which was first effectively discovered by Thomas Clarkson and became an important political weapon in the campaign to discredit and then to end the slave trade. It is symptomatic that a contemporary sailor's song warned of the dangers:

> Beware and take care
> Of the Bight of Benin:
> For one that comes out
> There are Forty go in.[35]

Landfall in the Americas did not mean the end of the slaves' sufferings, but merely another round of new humiliations followed, if the slaves survived, by a lifetime's labour. The sale of slaves varied greatly. In general the slaves had to be 'prepared' for sale; cleaned, shaved, spruced up and, in the case of those suffering from stomach ailments, quite literally bunged up. The whole exercise was designed to enhance their physical appeal (and hence their value), to make them look younger, healthier; grey hair – often acquired on the voyage – was sometimes dyed. Factors and agents boarded the ship to inspect the human cargoes, setting in train a familiar pattern of advertisement and sale. Indeed it was similar to a modern rural market day. The goods (that is, the slaves) were widely advertised in the press and handbills and the sale carried out on a certain designated day before an assembly of interested onlookers: overseers, planters, agents, trusted slaves and the merely curious. In parts of the Caribbean the slave sales took the form of the 'scramble', where, at a given signal, purchasers rushed among the assembled (and terrified) slaves and tried to gather the ones they wanted. Rarely, however, was a whole cargo sold instantly, despite the demand for black labour. The price of the slaves, their physical condition, availability (or acceptability) of credit and the complexities of international bartering, all could delay the disposal of a slave cargo. When the *James* arrived in Barbados in May 1676, the sale was protracted, as the captain recorded in his log:

Tues. May 23rd	Orders to prepare the slaves for sale on Thursday
Weds. 24th	Our slaves being shaved I gave them fresh water to wash and palm oil and tobacco and pipes
Thurs. 25th	Mr Steed came on board to sell our slaves – we sold 163 slaves
Friday 26th	We sold 70 slaves
Sat. 27th	Sold 110 slaves
Monday 29th	Delivered 80 slaves which were part of the 110 sold on Saturday
Thursday 30th	Went on board with a planter to sell him some of our refuse slaves but he did not take them . . .
Wednesday 31st	Mr Man and myself came on board and sold five of our refuse slaves.[36]

It is hard to imagine a worse degradation; the old, sick or injured were simply 'refuse', unwanted and of little economic value. The slave traders simply wanted to get rid of them but slave owners could find little use for them. Indeed it was a frequent complaint from the North American colonies in the eighteenth century that the slave traders kept merely the unwanted slaves for the northern colonies, preferring to sell their better slaves in the more profitable islands at earlier ports of call in the Caribbean. This was, from a business viewpoint, perhaps natural enough on those slave ships which sailed onwards to the mainland (notably to Virginia). There were other slave ships, however, which brought African slaves direct to the northern colonies. But whatever route the slave ships took, in their acquisition of slaves the North Americans, in the mid- and late eighteenth century, found cause for complaint. They were aggrieved by the price, condition, numbers, times of arrivals and conditions of credit – all of which fuelled the growing American economic resentment at the British colonial dominance and which helped to pave the way for the evolution of American independence in 1776.[37]

26. A slave auction in New York in the seventeenth century

The slave trade was thus responsible for the demographic transformation of parts of the Americas and for the enrichment of the slave traders, white settlers and vested interest groups in Europe. In fact the problem of the slave trade's profitability has troubled historians for some time. Earlier critics suggested that the trade was largely responsible for Britain's pre-eminent economic position in the western world by the late eighteenth century, and perhaps even underpinned the nation's ability to become the world's first

27. A slave auction

industrial power.[38] Such claims are now generally thought to be greatly exaggerated and it is important to remember that the slave trade, important as it was, was only one of a large number of maritime trading routes which generated trade and wealth for Europe in her dealings with Africa, Asia and the Americas. Equally it needs to be pointed out that England's main maritime trade and source of wealth was trade to and from Europe.[39] Moreover, even if we choose to consider only the trade with Africa, historians of the slave trade have tended to overlook the remarkably diverse types of trade which lured the Europeans to Africa. In the words of Philip Curtin, 'In almost every part of the continent, the slave trade was only one among a number of currents of long-distance commerce'.[40] It is also clear that the earlier claims about the levels of profits made through the slave trade have been greatly inflated. More recent work suggests a much humbler, less spectacular rate of profit as an average return.[41] But this is not to deny the *expectation* of high profitability; the hope and aspiration by European investors in the trade that their gamble would yield a lucratively high return. Such hopes were occasionally realised. More often than not, however, slave-trading profits were modest and much in line with other areas of economic speculation.

Even to enter this argument may seem to some to be a cynical exercise in overlooking the gross misfortunes of the Africans and it would certainly be wrong to conclude this brief survey by concentrating on the slave traders. Millions of Africans were plucked from their homelands; millions died *en route*; generations were consigned to a lifetime's bondage – a bondage which they were then obliged to bequeath to their children and to successive generations. Once in the Americas, the slaves were put to work, treated as beasts of the field, and all for the advancement of their white owners. This, then, was the heart of the matter. The African slaves had become 'things' in order to aid the material wellbeing of their captors and owners. To that end the Africans were set to work.

5. Slave Work

Africans were transported across the Atlantic to work. In the early years of colonisation they were expected to undertake the onerous tasks of breaking open the virgin lands; cutting, burning and clearing the bush and rendering the land cultivable and habitable. Such tasks, shared by black and white alike, free and unfree, required brute strength. But in that early phase Africans were no

28. Slaves clearing a forest in Brazil

more or less important than indentured workers, or indeed the white land-owners. With the economic specialisation attendant on the transformation of the land, notably the evolution of plantations from the earlier small-holdings, black labour became vital. Indeed, without the infusions of African slaves the transformation of certain parts of the Americas would have been impossible. This was especially true in the tropics where the plantations flourished on cheap labour, a luxuriant climate and the growing European demand for tropical produce. The plantation system stimulated black slaving – and hence the slave trade – on an unprecedented scale. And to utilise and maximise black labour to its fullest, new systems and organisations of labour were devised. The plantations were marshalled and regulated in a fashion which, though perhaps

29. A field negro on a sugar plantation

common in the mines and, at a later date, in the early industries, was quite unusual in the seventeenth and eighteenth centuries. Indeed black labour was sorted and worked, regulated and marshalled very much in an industrial style, though their activities were primarily agricultural.

Men and women, young and old, healthy and infirm were shuffled into various groups of economic usefulness. The healthier, stronger slaves were herded into the field gangs whose tasks during crop time and planting, tended to be the most onerous. Other gangs were composed of less strong slaves in proportion to the necessary degree of physical effort. The least exacting tasks – of attending the animals, cleaning up fields and paths, supervising the pens or merely guarding animals or property at night – fell to the young, the old, or the infirm. It is characteristic that when slave holders took stock of their slaves, the slaves' health was often described in *economic* terms: 'old and useless'.

As the sugar plantations became more sophisticated, the complexity of their labour demands developed accordingly. To process the sugar cane, the plantation factories needed a nucleus of highly skilled slaves – boilermen, coopers, blacksmiths, masons and carpenters – all of whom contributed vital artisnal skills which must have been beyond the ken of most freshly imported slaves. Similarly there grew up around the white elite a veritable army of black retainers – cooks, nannies, servants, gardeners and concubines – all of whom filled the whites' houses to the brim. Indeed the number of black servants attending the slave owners was normally out of all proportion to the basic needs of the whites. It was however an indication of a man's wealth and status that he could surround himself with such trappings of luxurious life. Naturally enough, those slaves with the qualities (real or imaginary) likely to appeal to the whites as ideal for domestic service, were distinctive and not necessarily possessed by all slaves. The benefits of life in the Great House were, in general, substantial and outweighed the well-known disadvantages of being under the minute supervision of white owners, more especially, it was thought, in the hands of a spiteful and oppressive white woman.

Plantations, particularly the bigger ones with upwards of 500 slaves, were in effect complete communities; settlements of population which dotted the fertile regions of the tropical landscape. But these were unusual and artificial communities in which the very great majority were black, enslaved and kept in place and at work by a small band of white owners, managers and overseers – and elite slaves. So imbalanced was the racial divide that fear alone and the threat of savage reprisals (however often put into effect) were not

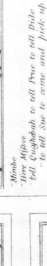

30. 'West India Luxury', a caricature of plantocratic life-style

sufficient to maintain stability, to say nothing of holding the system together. Despite the well-known and frequent slave resistance, black slavery was an unusually stable system but it survived thanks to an indefinable web of social and psychological forces operating on the slaves, both individually and in the mass.

Work itself was used as a prime instrument in maintaining peace and stability among the slaves. Throughout the history of black slavery, slave owners were uniformly in agreement that idle or unemployed slaves were potentially dangerous. It is also true that, even in Europe in the seventeenth and eighteenth centuries, the ruling orders expressed serious reservations about the unfettered leisure lives of their social inferiors, but in the slave colonies the stakes and the alternatives were so much more stark and alarming. Thus the fear of 'idle hands' was all the more acute among slave holders. There was another side to this: from the first, slave owners justified slavery in terms of the blacks' natural laziness; it was, they claimed, only the restraints and coercions of slavery which kept the slaves at work and prevented the outbreak of endemic black resistance. It was no easy matter to keep the slaves at work. Planters in particular faced serious problems for, like all forms of

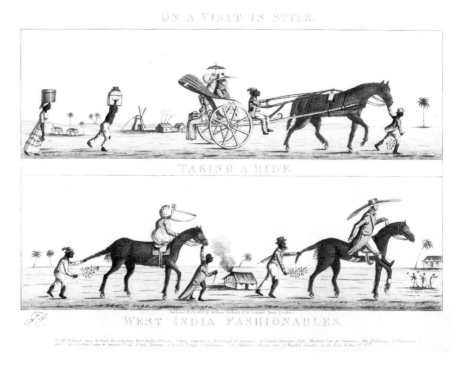

31. 'West India Fashionables', a caricature of the West Indian slave owners

agricultural work, plantation work, whether in cotton, sugar or coffee, involved periods of relative idleness. Whereas a farmer using free paid labour could always lay off his harvest workers, the slave owner was obliged to find permanent work for his captive labour force. This is one of the key arguments advanced for the inefficiency of slave labour: it simply did not maximise the labour potential of the slaves. Like military service, slavery created a routine of often pointless, time-consuming tasks simply to occupy the slaves in those periods of the year (upwards of six months) when the natural rhythms of the local crop created plenty of free time. The converse is however true; namely that in crop or harvest time, life for all the slaves could be hellish and demanding. Strenuous work, from dawn to dusk (sometimes even longer if slaves had to walk long distances to the fields), short breaks, exacting tasks in the fields or factories, the need to meet deadlines or to synchronise work with other groups of slaves; these and many other features drained the slave community of their collective strength. While most planters realised that brutality was counterproductive, slaves ran the ever-present risk of falling victim to the personal or savage whim or dislike of a white overseer or a slave gang ieader. Too much emphasis has been placed on the whip as an instrument in the control and work of the slaves in the Americas. Nonetheless it was both a threat and often a reality, frequently wielded capriciously and for no good cause.

Rather than beat slaves into submission, planters were preoccupied with the best ways of governing them via careful regulation of their work. Scribes and supporters of slave owners wrote numerous manuals and guides designed to offer instructions about the difficult task of learning to regulate and to work the slaves. How to control and cajole the slaves was as important as the complex agricultural and horticultural problems of tropical farming.[1] But the nature of slave work, and hence, the problems of slave 'management' varied greatly between types of crop. Sugar was in many respects the most demanding of large-scale slave employments; rooted in a necessarily oppressive climate, with a pattern of harvesting and processing which was physically exacting, the sugar plantations inevitably imposed a harsh routine on the black labour force. This was less true for other crops. Tobacco farming demanded fewer intense periods of heavy work and, like other crops (rice, cotton and coffee, but unlike sugar) tobacco did not require immediate processing. Moreover the economies of these various tropical crops – sugar excepted – were varied and in slacker periods the slaves could be redirected to food cultivation. Thus what so often made bondage better for particular slaves was the kind of work they were obliged to do. And at the heart of that problem lay the nature of economic development of a particular crop or region.

32. Planting cane

33. Cutting cane

From William Clarke, *Ten Views in the Island of Antigua* (1823)

34. Crushing cane

35. The boiling house

From William Clarke, *Ten Views in the Island of Antigua* (1823)

Slaves seem to have fared worst when faced by frontier and pioneering conditions, when white settlers forced the slaves to endure the privations of frontier life and harsh working conditions. In the case of Brazil, for instance, earlier historians argued that local slavery was unusually benign, but it now seems clear that there were marked brutalities to the slaves whenever and wherever certain crops or regions were in an expansive phase.[2] This aside, even the apparently less-demanding crops could provide a miserable environment for the slaves. Local laws, the countervailing pressures from churches or other outside bodies (which sometimes tempered the cruelties shown to slaves) were swept aside by the economic needs of the moment. This, for instance, is what happened in the sugar boom on the French island of St Domingue in the late eighteenth century and during the resurgence of slave-grown sugar and coffee in Brazil and Cuba in the nineteenth century.

From all the slave colonies a stream of descriptive accounts found their way back to Europe, documenting the horrors and miseries of slave life and work. Some accounts, however, told a contrary story; of a less hostile environment not much worse – if at all – than that endured by Europe's oppressed peasantry. But too often these benign views of slavery were of *urban* slavery and domestic slavery. While it is tempting to think of slavery as a largely rural phenomenon, there was a notable urban slave experience. The towns throughout the Americas attracted large numbers of slaves and their lifestyle and work tended to be quite different from those of their rural peers.

Towns in the eastern Americas and the Caribbean were particularly important as entrepôts for communications of people and goods between the old world and the new. It was through the seaport towns that the slaves arrived and had their first glimpse of the Americas. Because of the important trading and service function of the towns and ports their economic activity attracted and encouraged a great deal of local slave labour. Slaves travelled to the towns from the rural interiors in charge of transportation, carrying goods for export and returning with the basic imported necessities which were so often the life-blood of the hinterland rural communities. In the ports themselves, for instance, slaves worked on the wharves and ships, attending to the myriad tasks of thriving maritime trade. Similarly, those white slave owners, planters, merchants or traders whose livelihood took them to or depended upon the towns and ports, had slaves working in their town houses. There thus evolved sizeable urban black populations, large numbers of whom lived under their owner's roof but many others were allowed to live separate lives in designated places. Although small scale, there developed distinct and notable groupings of black slaves some of whom could hire themselves out as labourers in the towns.[3]

In the US South, the very great majority of slaves in the early nineteenth century lived on plantations or in rural occupations. Indeed it is often argued that it was the relative failure of the South to urbanise which was largely responsible for the region lagging behind the North. Nonetheless, in those towns and cities which dotted the South, slaves were to be found in abundance. Moreover the economic diversity of town life provided opportunities for urban slaves which were quite beyond the reach of their rural peers. Slaves in New Orleans, for instance, are perhaps best remembered of all

36. Slaves for sale in New Orleans

when they appeared on the auction blocks on the New Orleans slave markets and were herded in slave 'jails' or 'yards' awaiting sale. But there were in addition many thousands who lived and worked permanently in the city; as many as 18,000 in 1850.[4] These slaves, unlike those on the tropical plantations of Brazil or the Caribbean, were owned not in large numbers but in very small groups indeed. In fact in New Orleans one-third of slave holders owned only one slave and half owned two or fewer.[5] The largest group of urban slaves worked as domestics but others filled a variety of functions in the towns: as porters, labourers and drivers. Others worked in the cotton industry or as dockers for the flourishing river trades. Local authorities devised a structure of laws and regulations designed to limit and restrict the movement and activities of local blacks, but it was equally obvious that many such laws would be broken or unenforceable. The end result was that in general slaves in New Orleans found themselves much less restricted than their peers in the country. Of course this argument might equally be applied in Britain in the same period; urban life often entailed a laxity of individual movement and behaviour which proved more difficult in rural society.

New Orleans was an old established city and its pattern of slave holding might be expected in a city which occupied so special a role in the Southern economy. But even when new urban areas evolved in the South – Baton Rouge, for instance, after 1808 – slaves became a prominent group in the town. By the time of the Civil War almost one quarter of the town's people were slaves. There, as in New Orleans, slaves played an important role in the local economy not merely as objects and chattels of trade, to be sold and bartered, but as creators of wealth. Slave holders hired out their black labour wherever the need arose, using blacks as a source of income. Other slaves were permanently employed in local industries[6] but the largest group were, as elsewhere, used as domestics. It seems natural that those Southern slaves who sought complete freedom from their bondage should flee north of the Mason–Dixon line. But the fate of the runaway and free black in the North was not a happy one. Even in Philadelphia (in the eighteenth century the second largest city in the British empire) whose free black population in 1860 was 22,000 – the largest outside the South – free blacks endured conditions of poverty and general immiseration.[7] Indeed the very forces which in the nineteenth century transformed the USA into an industrial giant, failed to enhance black life because of what has been described as the 'institutional racism and structured inequality' confronting blacks throughout urban America.[8]

Wherever we look it seems clear that when Southern slaves lived in towns and cities they experienced – or created for themselves – an element of social and economic freedom which was beyond the reach of their rural peers.[9] Still, on the eve of the Civil War the very great majority of Southern slaves were rural. Occasionally, however, pockets of urban blacks provide a contrary and often distinctive picture of slave life and work. In Athens, Georgia, at mid-century for instance, almost half the population consisted of slaves, the bulk of them working as 'household servants, yard boys, gardeners, carriage drivers, and in other capacities in keeping with city dwellers'.[10] Here, as elsewhere there was a complex structure of local laws and regulations aimed specifically at controlling the movements and activities of local slaves. But in the absence of effective policing in the town, local slaves were free to do much as they wanted.[11]

37. A slave coffle in Washington in 1819

38. Slaves working on the land, with a view of Montgomery, Alabama, in 1860

It seems clear beyond doubt that, in the less tightly controlled world of urban life, slaves could find for themselves a flexibility of movement and an element of independence which was quite at variance with the more supervised lives of rural slaves. It was perhaps understandable that in such conditions of relatively lax control (for a slave society that is) many slaves would transgress the rules and expectations of the slave-holding class and find themselves in trouble with the law.[12]

If it is generally true that urban slaves fared better than their rural counterparts and were able to avoid the worst rigours of the laws designed to contain them, it still remains the case that, in relation to their owners, they stood in much the same position. It was the black who tapped the economic potential of the slave-holding regions, be it Southern cotton, Caribbean sugar or Brazilian coffee. Even when the slave-owning town dweller owned merely one or two slaves, those slaves could still provide their owner with income from their labours.

As early as the mid-sixteenth century, a visitor to Brazil highlighted the working relationship between master and slave.

> As soon as persons who intend to live in Brazil become inhabitants of the country, however poor they may be, if each one obtains two pairs or one-half dozen slaves . . . he then has the means of sustenance.

The case of Brazil provides an excellent illustration of the variety of occupations and of the complex economic roles which slaves came to play in the burgeoning fortunes of the Americas. In the words of Leslie Rout Junior, 'Not only were they field hands, domestics, peddlers, miners, bodyguards, skilled labourers, and objects of sexual gratification, but also soldiers, overseers and thieves.'[13] Moreover, the kind of work slaves did determined to a large degree what free men (black and white) would not do; black labour thus became the marker by which non-slaves came to judge the suitability of certain tasks or occupations for themselves. Throughout Brazilian history, for three centuries from the mid-sixteenth onwards, the sugar planting economy was crucial. Some historians have tried to suggest however that the worst rigours of Brazilian slavery were alleviated by the friendly relations which developed between master and his black mistresses. In truth, and as in the British Caribbean, the great majority of field slaves remained utterly unaffected by the relations between black and white in the Great House. Whatever tender or affectionate feelings existed between slave owners and their mistresses, there is no evidence to suggest that these feelings were then passed on to the great mass of the slaves.

Brazilian sugar planters, like their Caribbean counterparts, provided only minimal diets for their slaves; they also knew that any shortfall in their labour force could be replenished via the slave trade. But the feeling that it was perhaps better and cheaper to buy rather than breed does not mean that planters wilfully destroyed or debilitated their slaves. But it undoubtedly compounded the strictly

39. Slaves washing for diamonds in Brazil in the eighteenth century

economic view of the slaves; by reinforcing the perception of the slaves as mere chattels replaceable through the normal channels of international trade. Furthermore, this view was often confirmed by leaving the plantation in the hands of minor white officials in order to allow the owner to 'retire' to the cities on the Brazilian coast, just as Caribbean planters returned 'home' to Britain. Slaves under the supervision of overseers or managers could normally expect more arbitrary and less sophisticated treatment than when their owner was close to hand. When the Brazilian planters did retreat to the cities however, they took with them numbers of slaves. Thus in Brazil, the Caribbean and in the US South there were substantial pockets of urban slaves.

Sugar was not Brazil's only valuable commodity. The discovery of gold unleashed that frenzied rush for instant wealth which was to occur at a later date in California and the Yukon. In Brazil the appalling work of mining the gold (and other precious metals) predictably soon became the preserve of the black slave. The mines became a mecca for thousands of European prospectors and speculators, and the destination for legions of black slaves who were funnelled into the region in unprecedented numbers. The mines exacted a fearful toll of slave life; and inflicted permanent damage to the health of many of those who survived its fatal consequences.[14]

Brazilian slaves could be found in the most diverse and varied of tasks and occupations. In the cattle-breeding areas, slaves were used as stockmen and cowboys (as indeed they were to be in the USA in the nineteenth century). They also worked in coffee, cacao and cotton productions, their conditions of labour varying, again, with the intensity of local economic activity. Slaves were even dispatched to the cold southern reaches of Brazil (though normally as a punishment for offences committed elsewhere). There they became a sizeable group among the workers in beef-breeding and meat production.[15] Throughout the varied economic activities in Brazil the imported Africans and their descendants were central to the development, expansion and success of white enterprises. Black slaves, skilled and unskilled, male and female, contributed to Brazilian development and wealth by the range of labours and skills they invested, however unwillingly, to the Brazilian economy.

Perhaps the most popular and widely known image of the black slave is the cotton worker in the American South. Yet slave-grown cotton on a mass scale was a relatively late development. At the time of American Independence (1776) slavery in those mainland colonies was perceptibly declining. But it was given a new lease of life by the invention of Eli Whitney's 'cotton gin' which revolutionised cotton production and stimulated the massive boom in cotton growing throughout a band of southern States from South Carolina to Texas. In 1791 the USA produced only 0.4 per cent of the world's cotton; by 1860 it produced 66 per cent.[16] The industrial north-east of the USA and the mills of Lancashire devoured this slave-grown cotton, spitting out in return those textile goods which clothed the western world throughout the nineteenth century. As American cotton boomed, so too did American slavery. But it was the country's economic good fortune (unlike the Caribbean or South America) that this geographic and economic expansion of slave-based work could take place without recourse to the Atlantic slave trade (ended in 1808). In the early nineteenth century, US slaves kept up – and increased their own numbers. In fact they doubled between 1810 and 1860 to four millions. Nowhere else in the hemisphere had such expansion taken place without massive importations of Africans. An even sexual balance, high birthrate in the older slave states and less taxing work in cotton – all of these factors and more cumulatively produced a unique pattern of slave reproduction.

40. Cotton picking in the Southern USA

While it is possible to describe in broad outline the main work undertaken by slaves, it is important to recall that slaves were scattered throughout the various slave societies. So numerous were they and so ubiquitous in certain societies that it was inevitable that many would even find their way into non-slave occupations. As we have seen some worked as cowboys, others, like Equiano, were sailors. Some became musicians and show men and women and artistes of various kinds and abilities, a tendency greatly accentuated by the growth of a free black population in the years following the ending of slavery. It is equally interesting to note the diversity of slave work and this was true for both men and women and for all ages. While slave holders had marked preferences for certain types (or tribes) of slaves and normally for healthy young men, female slaves were no less important. Indeed women outnumbered men in many areas of the most onerous field work at the height of slavery. Clearly the sexual favours demanded of slave women gave them dubious opportunities for their own material improvement – and that of their offspring. Certain jobs, particularly on the plantations, were set aside for women slaves. Cooks, domestics, hospital workers, child-minders (all in addition to heavy field work) were the effective monopoly of female slaves. In fact it seems that the only slave work not generally undertaken by women were those skilled artisan crafts which normally passed from father to son. Many slave women, as we have seen, became concubines and common-law wives of white masters. Sometimes this took place against their wishes – and the wishes of their slave menfolk – with incalculable damage to the emotional lives of those concerned. For many years historians have argued (as did many contemporaries) that family life among the slaves simply could not and did not exist. We now know that this is not true and that, to the contrary and despite powerful countervailing social and economic forces, slave families were the norm. It is likely however that the role traditionally assigned to the man, as producer and protector of the wider family, was seriously jeopardised and even eroded by slavery. In its turn this placed a great onus on slave women – on mothers, grandmothers, aunts and sisters – to act as the cohesion to family life. Put crudely (while being aware of the obvious manifold exceptions) slave women played a pre-eminent role both as unifiers of family life and in the wider economic activity of their particular slave community. Yet for all their economic value to the life of community, slave women were perhaps even more important in shaping and holding together the social fabric of slave life as it evolved beyond the ken and the control of the slave holders.

Slavery was not a static institution and to gain a full picture of slaves' working lives we need to imagine the full life cycle of any individual slave. From the moment an African arrived in the New World or was born into slave society there, life thereafter was a more-or-less continuous commitment to work; the prospects of good luck, of manumission or of securing a privileged job were remote in the extreme. A child slave would be put to work as soon as he or she could be entrusted with simple, undemanding jobs, thereafter graduating through different tasks, depending on age, strength and skills, until old age or infirmity thrust the slave back down through the slave social structure. It is characteristic that we find aged or sick slaves joining forces with the very young in work they had first done in their own childhood. Of course this picture is in many respects a composite picture but it is one which represents a real and actual life history; a scale of limited experiences and expectations for millions of Africans born to serve their owner's interests.

This bleak description, however accurate, is not to suggest that the slaves were utterly crushed by their work. Some no doubt were. But it is the vitality of slave responses, the richness of their social lives and the inescapable fact of individual and collective resistance to their bondage which are, on closer investigation, more striking than their subjugation to a debilitating regime.

Despite everything, despite enslavement, the Middle Passage, the human losses in the seasoning period (the years immediately after arrival), the lifetime's work and personal upheavals; despite the disease, poor diet, abject material conditions and arbitrary cruelties; despite all these and more, slaves were able to create for themselves a fabric of much fuller social and personal life than observers could possibly have expected or even detect.

6. Social Life

Despite the slave holders' efforts completely to control and regulate their slaves' lives, the slave communities naturally evolved a wide range of social activities. There was a vast range of customs, habits, pleasures and behaviour about which the slave holders knew very little indeed, though they suspected and feared. Autonomous and independent slave life was not something which slave owners approved of. For the slaves however, their life away from work and the master's gaze provided a haven away from all those oppressions and indignities heaped upon them; an antidote to the daily routines carried out to the instructions of the white owners.

Once work was done – and even, at times, in the midst of work – at festivals and holidays, at family, tribal or communal celebrations, slaves embarked on their own private customs and pastimes. In physical terms this was quite easy since most slaves normally lived in separate quarters. They lived in their own villages, in slave 'pens' or yards or, if in domestic work, in huts and buildings clustered close to but separate from the masters' houses (close enough to be on call but distant enough not to make the whites feel uncomfortable). Clustered together, in family groups, with relatives, offspring, friends or in the midst of a sizeable slave community, there was ample opportunity and reason to seek personal or collective diversion. And from Africa, the slaves imported into the New World brought experiences, memories and cultural forms which, in conjunction and fused with certain elements of local white culture, developed into patterns of non-work behaviour which, though distinctively enslaved and black, varied greatly between the different slave societies.

A great deal of social activity depended on the family for, from an early stage, slaves organised themselves into family units. Many, if not most of the mature slaves had been wrenched from existing family relations in Africa. But the re-creation of family life in the teeth of adverse conditions was one of the truly remarkable feats of slave society. Where modern demographers have been able to penetrate the myths and uncertainties about slave family life it is clear that the great majority of those families were nuclear families.[1]

82

41. Slaves at leisure, 1861

Those slaves who did not belong to such families tended to be Africans whose lives had been completely disrupted by the slave trade. This was true in the British Caribbean and was no less the case among slaves in the US South, notwithstanding the powerful economic and migrational pressures which tended towards the destruction of family life.[2] And it was from the crucible of family life that so many facets of slave culture evolved. Within the home, however mean or squalid, slaves acquired many of the most important of cultural lessons: of child-rearing, cooking, loyalty to family, tribe or, later, to the wider slave community. It was from within the family that the practical lessons of survival in the hostile world were bequeathed from parent to child and where the folk stories, songs and customs of an African past were woven into the cultural inheritance of slave children born into slavery in the Americas. There too beliefs were adopted, whether of a religious or more secular nature. In sum, it was within the family home, inside the slave quarters that Africans and Afro-Americans evolved their unique social and cultural systems.

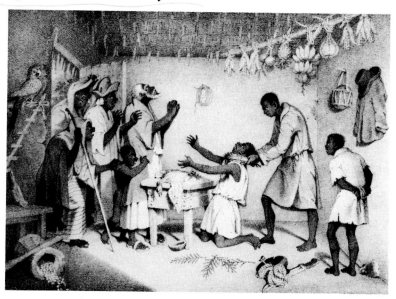

42. 'Negro Superstition', a slave ceremony by Robert Bridgens

White men feared the slaves' religions above all else, condemning them (until the relatively late arrival of Christianity) as unfortunate survivals of African barbarisms. Yet those religions varied enormously, and sometimes, unusual as they seemed, were perhaps the single most important intellectual and social framework among

the slaves. Here there was an often direct link to the severed
homelands of Africans and an explanation for the appalling
experiences suffered by the slaves. Equally, slave religions provided
a solace in the midst of continual sufferings and offered the
prospects of happier times to come. White denunciations of slave
religions as mere superstitions must have seemed bizarre to those
slaves who saw at first hand some of the more peculiar features of
Christianity itself.

A wide range of African-based religions took root in the different
slave societies. And those beliefs offered more than simple worship.
Religions from West and Central Africa seem to have enabled the
slaves to resist the controls and the values imposed by the slave
owners.[3] With their own particular rituals and beliefs, and led or
dominated by men and women of prominence and even some
charisma in the slave community, these religions, notably myalism,
made sense of the slaves' present predicaments and offered
acceptable alternatives. Such religions afforded protection (through
charms and medicine)[4] offered a collective forum beyond the reach
of the master and often became an important force in shaping varied
and ever-present resistance of African slaves to their oppression.[5]
Some slave religions were more obviously African importations than
others, though normally in transmuted form. Others soon became
overlaid with prominent imagery and rituals used by the whites. This
was particularly striking in Catholic regions where the cult of saints
was often absorbed into African belief systems. From such a fusion
there emerged *voodoo* in Haiti, *shango* in Trididad, Recife, Grenada
and Venezuela, and *candambé* in parts of Brazil.[6] When Europeans
made deliberate attempts to impose their own religions on slave
societies in the late eighteenth century, the fusion of two distinct
cultural forms became even more striking. Many regions of the New
World, however, remained isolated from regular contact with
European influences. There in remote, mountainous island reaches
or deep in the inpenetrable regions in South America, older African
beliefs survived in recognisably African form. Of course where
direct contact with Africa continued, via slave importations, to a
much later date (as, for instance, was the case in Brazil and Cuba),
African religions and beliefs survived and were even strengthened as
Africans poured in from the slave ships. Whatever their form and
however obviously or unalloyed African they might be, such
religions offered more than mere 'superstitions' or escapist relief.
On the contrary, they provided an important social institution which
was amenable to slaves' interests and needs and provided the means
of creating an autonomous sphere of action in a harsh world which
was, ostensibly, totally controlled by their owners.

43. Family worship in South Carolina, 1863

Contemporaries tended to take slave religions seriously only when and if they became European and Christian. Indeed there has been an unfortunate ethno-centric habit of refusing even to regard non-Christian religions as religions at all. Nonetheless, various forms of Christianity did prove attractive to slaves. Until the later eighteenth century Catholicism was generally more in evidence among the slaves than the various Protestant churches, though this began to change with the emergence of non-conformist missionaries in the late eighteenth century in the Caribbean and North America. It has often been argued that the more forceful presence of the Catholic Church in Hispanic possessions resulted in more tolerant slave regimes in those areas. Recent work however has cast serious doubts on this argument. The Church in Spanish America was one of the largest of all slave holders though this did not prevent the Church from instructing large numbers of slaves in the basic tenets of Catholic faith. Whatever the shortcomings of the Catholic Church, their work was in marked contrast to the persistent failure – indeed the powerful resistance – of Protestant authorities to convert and instruct local slaves (and this despite the frequent plantocratic assertion that one virtue of slavery was that it rescued Africans from paganism; and despite the planters' deep distrust and fear of their slaves' indigenous faiths).

Whatever the dominant faith of slave owners, they shared a basically similar problem: how could they control the beliefs and social lives of their slaves, when those slaves were regularly augmented with fresh supplies of Africans? Particularly in remoter rural communities, the slaves were distant from the dominant master culture. And as long as the slave trade survived, it would transfuse into existing slave communities the complexities of beliefs and values derived from Africa. There were doubtless many features of the masters' faith and religious ceremonies which appealed to (or could be used by) those slaves who came into contact with them. But in general and certainly until quite late in the history of black slavery, it was African beliefs and customs, even in transmuted form, which formed the bedrock of slave religions. And for this reason alone, if for no other, they would be hated, feared and outlawed by slave owners who, despite their own relentless appetite for African labour, sought to purge their captive labour force of all traces and stains of Africa.

This was a plantocratic ideal, but one which rarely came to fruition. The most obvious manifestation of the attempt to strip slaves of their African heritage was the renaming process. This began on board the slave ships, when Africans were listed as mere cargo, given a number and denied their own names. John Newton recorded in his log:

Sat. Dec. 29th. At 2 a.m. the yaul came on board, brought six slaves, one woman, two boys and three girls, all small, No. 38 to 43.

Even in death the slave was designated by number and not by name.

Buried a man slave, No. 84 of a flux . . . This morning bury'd a woman slave, No. 47, know not what to say she died of, for she had not been properly alive since she first came on board.[7]

Once in the slave colonies, slaves were often renamed by their new owners and the more local-born a slave population became the more European (or at least, non-African) the slaves' names became. This was particularly true when Christianity began to make a fuller impact and when slaves began to adopt surnames, often borrowed from whites they knew.

Clearly an African's origins could not be destroyed simply by renaming. Planters were however more concerned about the strength of their slaves' tribal commitment and made determined efforts to separate slaves from similar tribal groups and allocate them to different working groups. There were obvious limitations to this policy especially when slave owners bought batches of slaves from one single tribe or region. Slave loyalties were not purely a matter of tribal links and could not easily be broken. It was widely believed that slaves transported on the same ship possessed a marked sense of kinship with each other (though this may also have reflected the fact that many had originally come from the same region). One British planter noted:

> we find that the negroes in general are strongly attached to their countrymen, but above all to such of their companions as came in the same ship with them from Africa. This is a striking circumstance: the term *shipmate* is understood among them as signifying a relationship of the most enduring nature.[8]

It is hard to see what planters could have done to destroy the cultures of Africa, or to erase the memories of the Middle Passage, as part of their overall ambition to deracinate their slaves and make them more malleable.

Throughout the history of black slavery there was a notable process of change at work, its pace varying from place to place. Stated crudely the African origins of slave society were gradually transformed, not merely by contact with European cultures – however indirect – but also by the necessary and inevitable process of adaptation to local work, environment, and to other local-born slaves. This process was most obvious in the case of language. The polyglot languages of imported Africans slowly gave way to (or were complemented by) local creole tongues: a simple necessity if slaves were to understand each other and their masters. This process varied enormously and on slave plantations which possessed a single or dominant tribal group, their particular language (often reflected in their names) could persist for a long time.[9]

African experiences found their way into countless features of slave society. Even slave work came to reflect that connection. Numerous Africans took to the colonies a range of skills – in metal and wood-working, for instance – which were important in a number of ways in local economic life. But the great majority of slaves were used as labourers, and while it may be thought that African agriculture may have provided a useful training for slave life the *nature* of slave labour was utterly different, a fact which so alienated the slaves. Driven like cattle to work and at work, slaves endured a regime of daily labour which was utterly alien to anything they might have known in Africa. However, some features of African farming and food production were of value in another respect, for in many cases slaves supplemented their diet by growing their own crops. On the whole, plantations tried to restrict their cultivable land for the production of their staple crops, but it was widely appreciated that to allow slaves their own plots and gardens would serve the double purpose of making the feeding of slaves less costly while occupying the slaves in their out-of-work hours. Here, in the 'Negro Grounds' slaves worked much as their African forebears, producing the foods which would have been recognisable and acceptable to Africans.[10] Indeed it is an indication of the significance attached to such independent provision grounds that, following slave disturbances, they were singled out for destruction by the white military, thus forcing the slaves back to even greater dependence on their owners. Giving evidence about Barbados to a Parliamentary Enquiry, the island's Governor noted that slaves were fed by their masters:

> except what they make from their own property of hogs, goats, fowls, which they are allowed to keep; and they have also a certain proportion of land allotted for their own use to plant provisions upon.[11]

Thus the agricultural culture and dietary habits of the slaves often looked remarkably African, though often taking on local forms.

Throughout the slave colonies, and also in Europe, it was widely assumed that Africans were peculiarly musical. Time and again commentators remarked on the role of music, song and dance in the cultures of Africans and among slaves throughout the Americas. Writing of Jamaican slaves in 1797 a commentator noted: 'Music is a favourite diversion of the Negroes; for the enjoyment of which they are well adopted by a natural good ear . . . .'[12] Music is an important expression of certain cultural forms in a host of different societies, but whites came to see something special and unusual in black music, assuming throughout that the blacks were naturally musical. It was undoubtedly true that slave music played an important role in slave societies, but whites made racial assumptions about what were primarily social characteristics. Even John Wesley notes: 'Negroes above all the human species I ever knew, have the nicest ear for music. They have a kind of ecstatic delight in psalmody.'[13]

A large number of African-styled musical instruments – wind, drums and stringed – found their way, in adapted form, into the slave quarters and soon became the essential accompaniment to most slave social gatherings, celebrations and festivals. Equally significant is the fact that slave owners associated slave music, particularly drumming, with slave resistance and violence. Slave songs often expressed powerful feelings. 'Satire, intrigue, the merit of a race and their own praise are the general themes.'[14] One commentator observed by comparison that 'Our lampoons, though delivered in better language seldom convey more poignant expressions of contempt'.[15] Indeed in the slaves' songs we are left with one of the few surviving direct expressions of slaves' languages, ideas and expression. Equally, in spirituals, jazz and other modern musical forms, the musical expression of the slaves has been inherited by the modern world.

Slave music permeated slave society. Work in the field was often accompanied by music and song. Field gangs and other work groups

44. A negro festival in St Vincent, engraved by Andinet after Ajostino Brunyas

working in unison at repetitive tasks frequently measured out the pace of their tasks and the rhythms of their work by singing; answers and responses to different tunes, the rhythmic beat of a particular tune, all helping not merely to complete the tasks and work, but providing a world within a world. Even in the midst of back-breaking effort slaves found a place for self and collective expression. This is particularly striking since many of those songs, at work or rest, mocked, denounced or insulted the whites, or expressed hopes, fears and anxieties. Communal or gang clapping, chanting and shouting, all gave the slaves a means of expression even when tied to the insistent demands of the master's work routines.

A good illustration of the process of cultural adaptation can be found in slave festivals. At Christmas, Easter and other European festivals slaves made the most of the opportunity offered them to relax and enjoy themselves; their collective endeavours often took a musical format. As with their owners, slave celebrations were normally an occasion for feasting and merriment. 'In imitation of their masters they sometimes make feasts, the expence of which is defrayed by a general contribution of the guests. On these occasions the best victuals are served and some liquors are produced in great plenty.'[16]

In the best traditions of pre-industrial European societies where specific provision was normally made for ritualised plebeian enjoyments, an occasion when the world was turned upside down and the normal codes and observances set aside, if only for the day, certain slave societies, or particular estates, permitted and even encouraged slave exuberance. At Christmas it was common to permit a 'Negro Ball' at which the whites danced with the slaves. In 1791 Sir William Young, visiting his estate in Barbados, met a 95-year-old slave who 'danced at the Negro-ball last Christmas; and I am to be her partner, and dance with her next Christmas'.[17] Another cause for major slave celebrations was the arrival of a visiting owner. Inspecting his Jamaican property in 1816, Monk Lewis remarked:

Whether the pleasure of the negroes was sincere may be doubted; but certainly it was the loudest that I ever witnessed; they all talked together, sang, danced, shouted, and, in the violence of their gesticulations, tumbled over each other, and rolled about upon the ground.

When his slaves came out to meet him, Lewis remarked on 'their strange and sudden bursts of singing and dancing'. Some days later, Lewis arranged a 'festival' and meal for his slaves and the evening was dominated by dancing and music.

Their music consisted of nothing but Gambys (Eboe drums), shaky-shekies, and kitty-katties; the latter is nothing but a flat piece of board with two sticks, the former is a bladder with a parcel of pebbles in it. But the principal part of the music to which they dance is vocal; one girl generally singing two lines by herself, and being answered by the chorus . . . The singing began about six o'clock, and lasted without a moment's pause till two in the morning; and such a noise never did I hear till then.[18]

In addition to such rare occasions, slave work normally allowed periods of rest and recreation, depending on the nature of the crop and the time of the year. But in the US South it was widely accepted that slaves ought not to work on Saturday afternoon and Sundays. And it was in those periods that formal slave leisures found their niche. Although appreciative slave owners realised the value – to themselves as well as the slaves – of permitting slaves a reasonable degree of leisure time, many took quite a contrary view and sought to curb slave recreations. The only obvious result of such impositions, however, was that slave enjoyments tended to be illicit and often subversive. As one US slave remarked: 'Ours is a light-hearted race. The sternest and most covetous master cannot frighten or whip the fun out of us.'[19]

Black slaves were materially poor and denied all but the basic essentials of life and as a result any musical instrument had to be improvised from whatever materials came to hand. Wood, string, animal bones and skin, gourds, cooking utensils, cans and sticks – all were used and converted to the never-ending need for slave music.[20] The most elaborate musical sessions, with mass singing, dancing and choral involvement, were to be found at set piece holidays, Saints' days and religious festivals, celebrations at the end of crop or harvest and, of course, Christmas and New Year. In the US South and in the Caribbean, slaves carefully prepared for Christmas holidays. 'The approach of the Christmas holydays is carefully noted by the negroes, most of whom make some provision for their being better dressed.' Slave women took inordinate time and money to dress themselves in the best available finery, despite the obvious expense.

The negroes from different districts in Guinea associate in parties and wander about the town, diverting themselves with their own peculiar singing, instruments and dances, the last of which they stop to perform.

Overall, the slave Christmas was noisy and turbulent:

the rattling of the chains and slings from the wharves, the mock-driving of hoops by the coopers, winding the postmens horns, beating militia and negroe drums, the sound of the pipe and tabor, negroe flutes, gombas and jaw-bones, scraping on the violin, and singing of men, women and children, with other incidental noises, make Kingston at this time a very disagreeable residence.[21]

45. An emancipation festival in Barbados

From these outbursts of slave pleasures, enjoyed publicly and collectively, there developed a number of carnivals some of which survive to this day. One of the most striking was the John Canoe parade in which slaves dressed in elaborate costumes and large painted masks to parade in long, noisy (and, to their superiors, troublesome) processions.[22] Practically every commentator on the West Indies made detailed comments on these slave carnivals; about the size, colour, noise and obvious importance to the slaves taking part. To dress themselves in such costly and elaborate finery clearly involved enormous time, and perhaps even more important, was very demanding of the slaves' severely limited resources. Designated as holidays by the slave owners, these festivals were taken over by the slaves, who imposed on them their own style and values and transformed them into distinctively slave celebrations.

More extended holidays, notably Christmas, were occasions for both black and white family gatherings. Slaves who were hired out or working away from their relatives made their way back to the plantations to join their families.[23] There were naturally limitations to this but even in its limited form it gives some insight into the importance of family life among the slaves and of the important amalgam which developed between black and white cultures. There were a number of contemporary critics who were well aware that such slave enjoyments might be construed as mere opiates; brief spasms of controlled pleasures to render more tolerable a life of unremitting toil. In the words of one critic of the US South:

On these days the chains of slavery with which the blacks are loaded and in which they toil unceasingly for their masters, are loosed. A smile is seen on every countenance and the miseries of the year seem amply recompensed by this season of hilarity and festivity.[24]

Similar criticism could of course be levelled at *all* those forms of slave enjoyments approved by slave holders. And while there is some truth in the allegation, it ignores the role of the slaves themselves who in fact effectively colonised these occasions and invested them with a uniquely slave style and significance to suit their own ends. In truth these major, periodic events were merely larger and more obvious manifestations of a much wider slave phenomenon: namely an independent social life conducted beyond the ken and control of the slave owners.

It may have been possible for slave holders to put controls and restraints on the more open forms of slave enjoyments. But what could they do about the large number of slave customs which were of necessity conducted in the home; in the hut, cabin or yard, far away from the gaze of the whites? A good illustration of such cultural forms were those customs slaves followed after the birth of a child, customs which were unmistakably African.[25] Planters tried to curb such customs (and perhaps, they felt, improve the infant's chances of survival) by establishing special lying-in hospitals or huts. It is also notable that burial customs also offered slaves an area of independent social activity outside their masters' reach. The deceased was laid out in state, dressed in available finery, with ornaments and trinkets committed to the coffin. There was often a slave wake, remarkably similar (at least in the response it evoked from hostile outsiders) to the Irish wakes in English cities at much the same time, with music, drinking and eating. Graveside orations, more music, ritual killings of animals and cooking the carcass and, again in African style, the leaving of food at the graveside for the deceased. The period of mourning was generally completed – perhaps a month later – by further graveside music, song and feasting.[26]

Slave owners feared potential unrest likely to be occasioned at slave funerals (which, in some colonies, were likely to be all too frequent, especially in the harshest of times). In the US South efforts were made to restrain 'excessive' slave funerals and replace them with supervised interment, a task made easier as more and more slaves became Christian. But the more solicitous slave owners realised that a suitable slave burial was important. Indeed manuals on slave management in the USA often made specific reference to the need to provide a decent and sensitive slave funeral.[27] Often however, the outcome was less than happy, forming but another reminder, if one were needed, of white indifference to black sensibilities:

When a slave die, he just another dead nigger. Massa, he built a wooden box and put the nigger in and carry him to the hole in the ground.[28]

There were more mundane and daily areas of slave life which effectively existed beyond the owners' control. This was true, for instance, even in the prosaic area of slave clothing. On the whole slave holders provided their slaves with the basic necessities of clothing and food and on the bigger plantations there were seasonal and ritual distributions of those commodities. Lengths of oznaburghs, baize, check and blanketing were distributed along with hats, caps and coats and certain utensils.[29] But in the last resort the slaves were left to convert these materials into their own clothes and their own foodstuffs. Basic clothing, extra finery, jewelry, elaborate headware, hairstyles, home-made sandals, these and other clothing and refinements were made by the slaves from very limited resources. Yet many contemporary accounts and illustrations tell

46. The burial of a family servant

quite a different story: of slaves neglected of basic dress, exposed to the rigours of harsh elements (hot and cold, wet and dry) and having to work in difficult occupations without the protection of proper clothing. When questioned about this, slave owners tended to describe the *ideal* provision of slave clothing and food; ideal but not typical.[30] What is perfectly clear is that it was the slaves themselves who made up the difference between basic necessities and a greater comfort; and it was they who provided whatever luxuries and refinements of dress and decoration they needed for personal or collective celebrations.

Much the same was true of slave food. Though provided with basic foodstuffs (though that, like clothing, could be withheld as punishment) the cooking and the supplementing of the diet was left in the hands of the slaves themselves. Owners provided fish or meat and certain root-crops or vegetables. But it was the produce from the slaves' own plots and gardens which alleviated the monotonous diet, adding a more balanced (and culturally more acceptable) dimension to slave nourishment.[31] Often slaves could supplement their diet by eating the crops or goods they were enslaved to produce. What is striking is that throughout the Americas slave food – home grown or allocated – was remarkably similar to much of that found in Africa. Yet at this point we confront a central problem of historical interpretation, for the diversity of slave experience was such that no generalisation can adequately convey the full reality. Those slaves owned by impoverished masters or living in harsh climates or locales would suffer accordingly.

Cooking, whether inside the hut or openly in communal style was generally done with implements which would have been familiar in Africa. So too were the eating utensils: the calabash cups or coconut shells, gourds, wooden and earthenware vessels, all homemade and clearly derived from African experience and usage.[32]

Perhaps even more hidden from the slave owners was the verbal culture of the slaves. At its simplest it was often difficult for masters to understand their slaves, even when they developed pidgin English, French, Spanish or Portuguese. Africans could hide their thoughts behind their native languages. Similarly Africa provided a myriad of folk tales which became so intrinsic a part and important a feature of slave life throughout the Americas. In Jamaica the Anancy tales were drawn directly from the Akan spider hero, Ananse, and were replete with stories of magic and spirits.[33] Folk songs too became a prominent feature of the slaves' cultural life. Satirical story-telling sessions were an attraction in the slave quarters in the evenings, at weekends or at high days and holidays. Time and again these stories tell of weaker creatures who outwit and outmanoeuvre their oppressors; how bullies and tyrants succumb to the ruses of their victims. These tales, told widely among slaves and even by trusted slaves to the whites' own faces, embraced humour and allegories at the heart of which lay morals directly relevant to the black slaves themselves. Not only were the folk tales recognisable to generations of slaves but their message, implications and moral conclusions were obvious and reassuring to all those slaves with an ear for the truth.

A fuller exploration of the social lives of the slaves would merely add voluminous detail to the kernel of this argument, namely that in the varied and multifaceted world of the slaves' social experience there existed enormous scope and potential for independent and autonomous slave activity. In some respects this may be thought to be a truism. Yet there is a temptation to consider slavery to be such an all consuming and utterly demanding institution which left little free time, energy or opportunity for even a rudimentary social existence. There were, undoubtedly, wretched slaves for whom this was true. But much more impressive are the countless examples of slaves who, despite the most adverse and abject of circumstances, created for themselves the essentials of an important and self-respecting social life. Moreover, in many aspects of this social life, the people who owned the slaves and who in theory controlled the slaves' every movement, were powerless. But in retrospect the evolution of a thriving social life among the slaves is perhaps even more significant as a reminder of the indomitable spirit, self-respect and communal feeling among people obliged to endure enslavement and bondage. It is when we consider the broader nature of the slaves' social lives that we begin to appreciate that the slave trade and slavery failed in its conscious attempts to dehumanise its millions of victims.

7. Resistance

47. A slave branding iron

Much of what has already been written about the slaves' social lives is a tribute to the levels of resilience to be found within the slave communities. In many areas of their lives they succeeded in putting a distance between themselves and their oppressors. But they also found varied and often ingenious ways of combating their enslavement in addition to their withdrawal into their private or collective social world. Throughout the history of slavery in the Americas slaves took positive and often highly effective measures to resist their enslavement; to make it less intolerable, to overthrow it or merely to frustrate and thwart their masters. Indeed the history of black slavery could be written in terms of the slaves' attempts to destroy or subvert the institution. The nature and incidence of resistance varied greatly between and within slave societies, but in all of them there are striking degrees of resistance falling short of open rebellion; personal or communal foot-dragging which hindered their owners' economic aims and gave slaves a decisive role in their own lives.

Rituals of resistance and a determination to advance self-interest or satisfaction by inflicting injury on an oppressor are not, of course, restricted to slaves. Similar responses can be found, for instance, among POWs, prisoners and even among people employed in monotonous industrial occupations in the modern world. Among

99

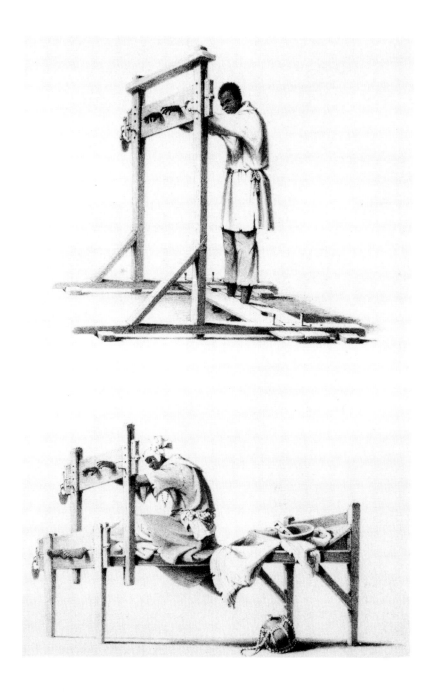

48. Slaves in stocks, from R. Bridgens

49. Bed stocks

the

slaves, however, this resistance often took on epic proportions and ranged from open and bloody violence through to subtle and almost indetectable tricks. It was, for instance, traditionally claimed that slaves were compulsive liars and thieves who would take any opportunity to steal their owners' goods and property. More often than not, slaves stole food and it seems reasonable enough to assume that the theft of food – then as now – has one prime and obvious purpose. Try as they might, through legislation and exemplary punishments, slave owners could not stop slaves from pilfering foodstuffs. Gardens were raided, crops stripped, animals killed and eaten, but unless such thefts got totally out of hand, slave holders were obliged to accept these depredations as part of their economic costs; a financial loss to be set against the other expenses of using slaves instead of free labour.[2] But in truth the theft of food was more likely to have been simply the response of hungry people.

In all slave societies, the white master class regularly accused their slaves of being congenital liars; almost unable to distinguish truth from falsehood (though traditionally using their lies to suit their own interests). Duplicity, said one Southern planter, 'is one of the most prominent traits in their character, practised between themselves, but more especially towards their masters and managers'.[3] This and even more extreme views were derived not merely from direct white experience of slaves in the Americas, but were informed by a host of racist misconceptions about black humanity in general. At the apogee of slavery it was widely believed and argued in educated white society that the black – free as well as slave – was possessed of some of the most unappealing antisocial characteristics. In the words of the *Gentleman's Magazine* in 1788:

> The Negro is possessed of passions not only strong but ungovernable; in mind dauntless, warlike and unmerciful; a temper extremely irascible; a disposition indolent, selfish and deceitful; fond of joyous sociality, riotous mirth and extravagent show.[4]

These and similar caricatured images were part of the slave holders' wider ideology and political purpose; to convince the outside world that only the restraints of slavery could keep such lawless people in check by imposing on them the necessary work discipline and rigorous social behaviour. It was also part of slave holders' efforts to argue that, despite their own sterling efforts, the endemic and natural vices of the blacks would periodically reveal themselves. In truth, hostile black responses made perfect rational sense to people who could see little or no reason to tell the truth or to refrain from stealing. There was an obvious vicious circle at work; a self-fulfilling prophecy on the part of slave owners who treated slaves in such a way that they often had little alternative but to behave in precisely the fashion so feared and hated by their owners. Hungry and deprived people stole; and why should they value the truth when, as so often happened, telling the truth merely plunged them and their friends into trouble? Slavery, according to one former US slave, 'makes its victims lying and mean; for which vices it afterwards reproaches them, and uses them as arguments to prove that they deserve no better fate.'[5]

While slaves obviously stole to satisfy their hunger, they also stole to thwart and frustrate their owners. In addition there was a marked degree of daily obstinacy among slaves in their working lives and there were never-ending complaints about slaves' inability to work regularly, consistently and properly – without compulsion. Slaves 'dragged their feet', working at their own pace and often failing to do a job properly. It was partly to overcome these problems that slave owners gradually devised a series of in-built benefits and perks to encourage slaves in a more vigorous and effective approach to their work. It seems rarely to have been completely successful. Inside the homes of the whites, where slaves were most closely supervised, black domestics were forever denounced for shirking, laziness and obstinacy.[6] But much the same was true of all forms of slave labour. Out in the fields there was the threat of physical punishment, but as fearful as this was it was ineffective – and even perhaps counterproductive – in persuading slaves to work properly. Though it is true that the history of slavery is littered with tales of physical outrages and attacks on slaves, corporal punishment is unlikely to have had the desired effect of forcing slaves to work harder and regularly.

If and when they chose, slaves could inflict damage or sabotage on their workplace. Setting fire to a cane field, ruining equipment, hobbling and poisoning animals; these and more were easily and perhaps temptingly available to the aggrieved and courageous slave. In the US South, arson and incendiarism were commonplace, just as violence against inanimate objects was widespread in Europe throughout the years of industrial and political revolution in the eighteenth and nineteenth centuries.[7] In slave societies, the punishment for any such act was fearful in the extreme but, as with open rebellions, this did not intimidate and prevent the slaves from risking their lives in order to strike a blow against the master. Sometimes their blows were direct and physical. Assaults on white people were, as we might expect, the most savagely punished acts of slave resistance and from the early days of slavery local laws and customs decreed swift and brutal punishment for the offending slave. In 1685 the *Code Noire* of the French islands ordered that:

> Any slave who has struck his master, his mistress or the husband of his mistress or their children to cause a bruising or bleeding, or on the face shall be punished by death.[8]

As slavery developed various legal measures were introduced to ameliorate slave conditions, but the right to exact the full penalty for black assaults on whites rarely wavered. Slave attacks were more common against their immediate white overseer rather than their owner, particularly on bigger properties, and were often prompted by a beating or ill-treatment, and were merely a normal human response to provocation and assault. Sometimes slaves planned the death or injury of a white. It was particularly remarked that slaves poisoned their white owners and often killed their children. Nor was this claim totally fanciful. Knowledge of poison, like other natural products, herbs, medicinal matters and drugs, was part of the African culture transplanted into the Americas. These in conjunction with whatever European poisons might be available were used to kill a particularly hated person. One Jamaican case involved a black servant girl of fifteen who admitted 'having infused corrosive sublimate in some brandy and water' after which she 'stood by the bed to see her master drink the poison; witnessed his agonies without one expression of surprise or pity'. Monk Lewis reported from the same island that one of his neighbours 'has now three negroes in prison, all domestics, and one of them grown grey in his service, for poisoning him with corrosive sublimate; his brother was actually killed by similar means'. Some masters were victims of a number of poisoning attempts, and there were even cases of planned wholesale poisonings.[9]

Poisonings were often difficult to detect, for in the tropics people – black and white – died suddenly and mysteriously from a range of sudden ailments. And slaves often poisoned each other.[10] Oddly enough the whites poisoned themselves – accidentally – by taking their own medicines often in a haphazard fashion to counter the attacks of their own self-indulgence or disease. This was particularly the case with the use of mercury to combat venereal disease. Nonetheless, it is easy to imagine how whites, particularly those hostile or aggressive to their slaves might, when ill or dying, readily imagine that the slaves were the cause of their distress. Accusations of poisoning were perhaps more common than acts of poisoning.

Some historians have argued that the ultimate resistance to enslavement was suicide. Now it is clear that suicide among slaves on the slave ships was common, and that slave records in the Americas often tell of slave suicides. It is, however, impossible to assess the *motives* for those deaths. Suicide is not peculiar to slave society and there is no evidence either of the incidence or nature of slave suicide to distinguish it from other such acts of self-destruction. Slaves put an end to their lives for a variety of distressed reasons, not all of them necessarily peculiar or unique to slavery. Similarly it has been argued that the frequency of miscarriage or abortion among slave women is an indication of slave resistance; of women refusing to help their owners by breeding more slaves. These arguments, like those about suicide, are ultimately unconvincing – and unresolvable – if only because they hinge inevitably upon the motives of the slaves involved. A slave who miscarried is unlikely to have told why it happened, even if she knew. Much more likely is the fact that miscarriage and lost pregnancies were related to the interconnected problems of hard work continuing late into pregnancy, poor diet and physical care, and the general physical shortcomings of slaves. Indeed, it is perhaps surprising that the evidence does not record a *higher* incidence of miscarriage, not necessarily self-induced, but simply because of the appalling physical circumstances endured by slave women.[11] After all this was the case among plebeian women in Britain throughout the nineteenth century.[12]

So far slave resistance has been discussed as an individual or *ad hoc* phenomenon. But it was organised and violent resistance which more than anything else remained the slave owners' nightmare.

> The planter's dream doth plainly seem
> To point a moral deep.
> If you choose to whack a nigger's back
> You should never go to sleep.[13]

Time and again slave rebellions rocked, and in one spectacular case, destroyed slave societies. Despite their frequency and ubiquity, slave revolts were much less notable among US slaves and, despite a great deal of research, historians of North American slavery have failed to uncover slave revolts on the scale and impact of those in the Caribbean or South America. In the tropical societies, revolts – or the threat of them – form the history of slavery itself. From first to last, African, then local-born slaves burst into spontaneous or planned acts of violence on a small and large scale. In the US South

50. The arrest of Nat Turner, leader of the revolt in Virginia in 1831

slave resistance tended to take other non-violent forms (often highly effective). Only in Louisiana in 1811 did slave insurgents approximate the numbers (300–500) regularly to be found, for instance, in West Indian revolts. The most famous of all US revolts, led by Nat Turner in Virginia in 1831, mustered about seventy slaves. The insurrections of Gabriel Prosser (1800) and Denmark Vesey (1831) involved even fewer slaves. In the Caribbean many hundreds of slaves were caught up regularly in widespread violent acts, killing hundreds of whites and destroying property on a massive scale. The revolts were invariably followed by savage acts of retribution and massive and bloody acts of white reprisal against the slaves – guilty and innocent.[14]

It has been calculated that the average number of slaves involved in Jamaican revolts was 400 (though that may be too high). But in that country between the English settlement and the mid-eighteenth century scarcely a decade passed without a Jamaican slave revolt.

51. Public punishment of slaves in Brazil

Between 1730–40 there was one each year. In 1760 a major revolt attracted 1000 slaves, dominated by Akan-speaking slaves and led by Tackey. Indeed throughout the seventeenth and eighteenth centuries, slave revolts in the Caribbean were primarily *African* revolts, often Coromantee, and generally headed by a powerful charismatic leader but drawing its strength from a large body of alienated and vengeful slaves. This was true in Antigua in 1735 where a plot was hatched to kill the local Governor and the leading planters and to seize the island. The plan failed and some forty-seven prominent slaves were executed and others deported. Local whites thought it significant that the plot had been hatched in African ceremonies to the accompaniment of music and dance.

These insurgents were only the more extreme and comprehensive of a spectrum of uprisings. Between 1640–1713 there were seven major revolts in the English islands, with many more plots frustrated. The slaves were in no doubt of their fate if they failed. A plot in Barbados in 1675 resulted in six slaves sentenced to be burned alive, eleven beheaded and dragged through the streets. In 1692 others were hung in chains. In Antigua in 1687 one rebel was 'burned to ashes', others executed, while another had his tongue wrenched out and a leg cut off 'as a Living Example to the rest'.

52. Slaves on a treadmill

One major obstacle facing potential rebels on many of the West Indian islands was their geography. Some were so small and compact or crowded that (short of total destruction of white society) the islands afforded few escape routes. In Jamaica, however, with its mountainous, wooded interior which in places was impenetrable, the bush offered a sanctuary to generations of runaways, and a last desperate escape route for the unsuccessful rebel. Indeed in the early years of English settlement, slave resistance was largely shaped by the terrain itself. The English inherited from their Spanish predecessors 'maroon' communities, of ex- or runaway slaves living

53. A slave in chains

wild or in settled communities in the bush; 'behind the lines' as it were of English plantocratic settlement. For the best part of a century these communities were augmented by more runaways and English attempts to flush them out and eradicate them failed. Until a peace treaty of 1739 with them, the maroons were in effect a guerilla community in the heart of slave society. Furthermore, that treaty is significant in that a powerful colonial regime had been obliged to treat with former slaves and recognise their independence.

Similar maroon settlements could be found in other slave societies, and were in fact persistent features of those societies where geography and circumstances allowed.[15] Relations between maroons and the local slaves were often unhappy and uncertain, for the infusion of fresh runaways always threatened to bring upon the maroons the wrath and retribution of slave owners. A similar pattern unfolded throughout Spanish America. In tropical lowlands, on the east of the Caribbean and the Pacific or in the mountainous interior, slaves made their escape and often established independent villages and viable and thriving communities. The Spanish took measures to curb such developments, though much of their efforts were directed against those who aided fugitives. These and exemplary and horrible physical punishment of captured maroons failed to curb that basic urge to seek the freedom of the bush or the mountains.[16]

Many slaves ran away who did not (and could not) join the maroons. Throughout the history of black slavery there was a regular and apparently unstoppable 'leakage' of slaves who simply 'ran away'. But just as frequent as these escapes, were their pathetic failure, and punishment; time and again the documents tell of recapture and punishment, though often followed by further escape attempts by the same slave. In societies where blacks had to prove their freedom, it was difficult for a slave to survive on the run even in the dense and luxuriant forest and mountains of the Caribbean or South America. In some regions there were quite simply few or no hiding places. That did not, however, stop slaves from trying and some indication of the frequency of slave escapes can be gauged by the volume of 'runaway' advertisements which litter the pages of colonial newspapers.

RAN AWAY

From her owners, about the month of Sept. last, a short creole wench named

DILIGENCE, alias JUNK

has a large scar on her breast, occasioned by a burn, with a toe off each foot, for which she wears slippers. Speaks very slow and artful . . . (Kingston, *Daily Advertiser*, 29 January 1790)

ABSCONDED

from John Munro's wharf at this place, the 30th ultimo a NEGRO SAILOR MAN, of the Coromantee nation: he is about 5 feet 5 inches high, his face is furrowed with small pox marks, he has no brand mark, his back has got several lumps which in some manner resemble a bunch of grapes . . . he is artful, speaks the English, French, Dutch, Danish and Portuguese languages; of course it is thought he may endeavour to pass for a free man . . . (Kingston, *Daily Advertiser*, 7 June 1790)[17]

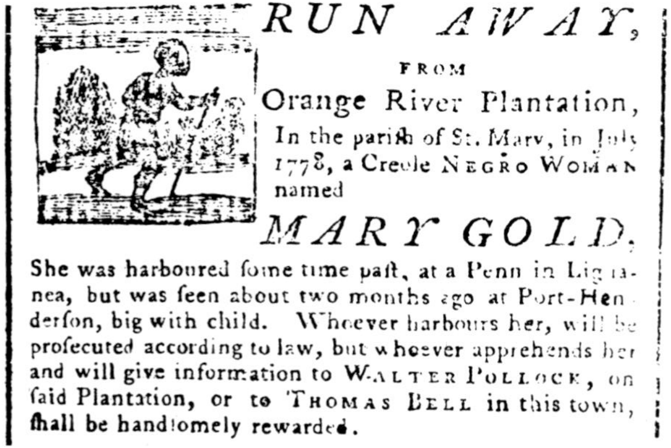

Kingston, Aug. 26, 1789.

RAN AWAY,

FROM the Subscriber yesterday evening, a NEGRO BOY of the Papaw country, named YORICK, with his country marks on his face, is about 4 feet 6 inches high, and had on a white shirt and no keen breeches. All persons are hereby cautioned against harbouring, concealing, or carrying him off, and whoever will bring him to me in Harbour-street shall receive a Pistole reward.

JAMES DAVENPORT.

834   Montego-Bay, Dec 14, 1790.

FOR SALE,

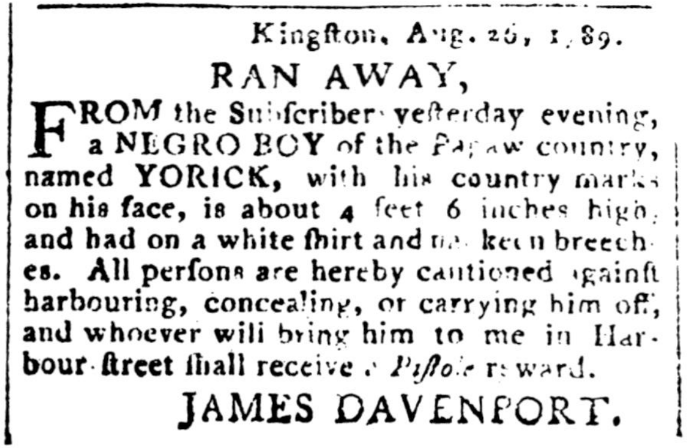

On Thursday the 23d instant,

439 Prime, Healthy, Young, EBOE

NEGROES,

Imported in the Ship

BROTHERS,

Captain JOSEPH WITHERS,

From BONNY.

James Wedderburn

RUN AWAY,

FROM

Orange River Plantation,

In the parish of St. Mary, in July 1778, a Creole NEGRO WOMAN named

MARY GOLD.

She was harboured some time past, at a Penn in Liguanea, but was seen about two months ago at Port-Henderson, big with child. Whoever harbours her, will be prosecuted according to law, but whoever apprehends her and will give information to WALTER POLLOCK, on said Plantation, or to THOMAS BELL in this town, shall be handsomely rewarded.

WANTED,

A NEGRO LAD,

Of the EBO Country, from 15 to 17 Years old,

WHO has had the Small-Pox, and is of a healthy Constitution. The Proprietor of such a Lad may hear of a Purchaser, by applying to JOHN PHILLIPS at his Shop near the Exchange.

54. Advertisements: runaway slaves and slaves for sale

55. Slave collar

Far more serious than escapes were the collective revolts. Whites forever felt that they were sitting on a powder keg, a feeling readily comprehended when we recall the ratio between black and white. In all but the American South, slave numbers rapidly overhauled the whites. Sometimes the slaves had a spectacular numerical superiority. Whereas in Barbados in 1660 the black–white ratio was roughly balanced (20,000 blacks to 22,000 whites) by 1713 blacks outnumbered whites by 45,000 to 16,000. Similarly in Jamaica, the balance of 1670 (about 7000 each) had changed by 1713 to 55,000 blacks against 7000 whites. In that same year in the Leeward Islands, 30,000 slaves greatly outnumbered the 9000 whites.[18] The coming of sugar instantly tipped the demographic balance the slaves' way. In Guadaloupe in 1671, 3083 whites faced 4267 slaves: by 1789 the 13,712 whites were faced by 89,523 blacks.[19] In Brazil in 1789 one and a half million slaves faced slightly more than one million whites: by 1818 it had grown to about two million blacks and 1,143,000 whites.[20]

These figures look even more spectacular when we recall that only in the US South did the slave population reproduce itself naturally: fewer than 400,000 slaves were imported into North America, yet by 1860 the black population of that region had become four millions. In Brazil, Jamaica and the other slave colonies much greater imports – sometimes on a staggering scale – failed to produce a self-sustaining population.

The ratio of blacks to whites was a constant and growing problem for the ruling groups in slave societies (who were often the very slave owners responsible in the first place for encouraging massive slave imports). Numerous laws were introduced insisting on a balance between black and white but with time the fines levied for failure to comply merely became a form of taxation. The stark truth remained that as long as the local economy demanded cheap labour, blacks would continue to swamp the master class (and their 'coloured' offspring with slave women). Hence the fear of slave revolt would persist.

In the light of these population figures it is perhaps surprising that slave revolts were not more frequent and successful. Furthermore, this is especially the case when we recall that slaves worked in their greatest concentrations on the plantations or mines where they had even greater numerical superiority than the national or average figures suggest. Towns and cities automatically tended to attract and keep a higher proportion of local whites who earned their living in the varied economic activities which serviced the rural interior or the trading links across the Atlantic. There were proportionately fewer whites in the country and consequently those whites living on, say, a plantation were vastly outnumbered by slaves. On Worthy Park in Jamaica in the late eighteenth century the black–white ratio varied between sixty-eight to one and thirty-four to one.[21] Moreover, such communities as Worthy Park were far from the nearest large white settlement, and there clearly developed a 'seige mentality'. Beleaguered whites could, it is true, call for assistance from other whites living on nearby estates, but they too were similarly outnumbered. In the event of slave troubles, military forces and the militia were normally miles – and many hours – away. Yet in the case of Worthy Park, and many other similar remote estates, there were, as far as we know, no slave revolts, a fact which cannot be explained solely by superior firepower or armaments. In crop time, for example, gangs of healthy young slaves were armed with a fearful array of cutlasses, axes and other agricultural implements. Despite their numerical superiority and at times their opportunities, slaves did not rebel here or in many similar situations. Many modern readers will find this odd and might find puzzling the ability of the outnumbered whites to maintain their violent and oppressive system in the teeth of such logistical and human difficulties. The same might also be said of feudal society which, like slave societies, survived for so long despite its manifest imperfections. Thus any analysis of slave revolts leads directly to the wider and more difficult problems of trying to explain the stability of slave societies.

There were various factors working in favour of the planters. The Middle Passage, the slave markets, acculturisation and the horrific death rates by disease not only devoured large numbers of Africans, but physically and mentally scarred millions of the survivors. Long before slaves reached their owners in the Americas they had undergone a traumatic experience which in part undermined their

resilience, willpower and self-confidence. This process was also
helped by the slave owners' attempts to break down the slaves'
natural grouping and to prevent the emergence of slave unity and
purpose. Equally there was the threat of physical punishment and
whatever limitations on the beating of slaves were laid down by local
laws, in reality slaves faced a ubiquitous threat from overseers, gang
drivers and masters. And for every slave who reared up in anger at
such assaults, there were many more who endured their pain and
humiliation with a stoicism which was doubtless seething and
scarcely contained.

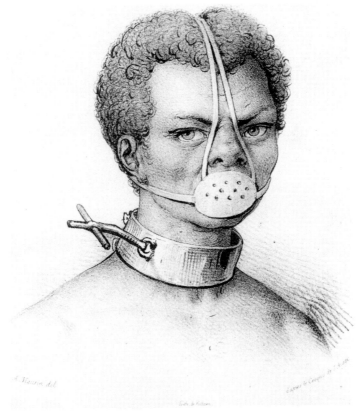

56. Punishment for a slave

It would be presumptuous for a modern historian to suggest that
slaves ought to have taken matters into their own hands more
vigorously. Who after all can feel confident of their own responses if
confronted by similar unimaginable circumstances? Moreover, to
suggest that slaves could have ended their oppression by rebellion is
to ignore the myriad ways in which they did indeed resist their

oppression. As we have seen, resistance short of rebellion was a daily and universal feature of slave societies and such tactics could not always be guaranteed to be free of painful consequences.

In only one case did slave rebellion bring about the destruction of slave society. And that case, in St Domingue (Haiti), was unique in the history of slavery in the Americas. From the mid-eighteenth century St Domingue had become the most recent 'boom' island of the tropical economy, its fertile lands and mountains attracting ever more waves of black slaves. The numbers of Africans deposited in Haiti in such a short period formed perhaps the most concentrated spell of re-population in the history of the African slave trade. In 1700 some 20,000 slaves had been settled there; by 1750 this had risen to 230,000 with the result that St Domingue was overtaking Jamaica as the world's main sugar producer.[22] On the eve of the French Revolution, so important had that island become that 90 per cent of the French slave trade was directed towards satisfying the island's gluttony for African slaves.[23] By then the island had become a byword for the quality, cheapness and volume of its sugar production – with all the inevitable economic consequences and dangers to the formerly all-powerful British sugar system.[24] But the emergent power of St Domingue, all built on the backs of its imported slaves, was shattered utterly by the ramifications of the French Revolution.

The ideals of 1789 – of liberty, equality and fraternity – had a corrosive effect on the French slave system based, like all others, on contrary ideals and practices. A decree giving free-born mulattos full civil rights created powerful resistance among whites on the island and their careless talk of independence and resistance to metropolitan France gave the slaves the opportunity to take matters into their own hands. Beginning in August 1791 a slave revolt wracked the island, killing numerous whites and devastating property on a major scale. When war broke out between Britain and France in 1793 the British (for a confusion of motives) despatched an army to St Domingue but they withdrew in 1797 having lost tens of thousands of men (most, it is true, to disease) and having failed to curb the black insurgents who were led in increasingly impressive and effective fashion by Toussaint L'Ouverture.[25] The French tried to reimpose colonial rule in order to rebuild the shattered economy but they failed, and independent Haiti was left to salvage what it could from a decade of bloodshed and violence.

Though it faced the new century as an independent, free black nation – the first in the colonial world – Haitian independence had been secured at a fearful price. The fate of Haiti, a poverty-stricken peasant society from that date to this, was grist to the slave holders' mill; an illustration, they claimed, of what black freedom must surely involve. More immediately, however, they saw in the violence of the revolt – of whites, blacks and mulattos killing each other with a ferocity which appalled even the hardest of planters – proof of what they and their apologists had always claimed and feared. In the

57. A modern drawing of Toussaint L'Ouverture

1790s when events in France cast a revolutionary shadow across the western world and even across the far-flung European possessions, the fear of revolution was not peculiar to the slave holders.[26] But Haiti offered a particularly savage and close-to-hand reminder to all slave holders in the Americas of the awesomeness of slave revenge and of the dormant potential for revolt. That the set of political and colonial circumstances which formed the vital initial conditions for the revolt were utterly unique, is much clearer now than it was at the time. Nor would an appreciation of this fact have proved of much comfort to other slave colonies. Revolutions after 1789 had the nasty habit of being contagious. How much more contagious might they be when experienced by slaves? Having said that, and despite the fear of contagion which in the 1790s became something of a psychosis among slave holders, there was never to be a slave revolt on the scale or success of Haiti.

At the time of the Haitian revolt there were other forces at work loosening the bonds of slavery. The growing European and North American critique of slavery, led by humanitarians, began to focus attention on the inequities and, later, the economic irrationalities of slave labour. One result of this emergent concern for slaves was the development of a missionary instinct (which hoped to bring 'civilisation' to the deprived slaves) and the proliferation of missions, notably non-conformist, in British slave colonies. Planters had traditionally feared and resisted slave conversion and those fears were to be fully justified. The major slave revolts of the early nineteenth century in the British West Indies (Barbados 1816, Demerara 1823 and most savage of all, Jamaica 1831) were all related to the demographic and religious changes at work among the slaves. With the ending of the British slave trade (1807) the islands became progressively less African and ever more Creole. At the same time the new churches provided growing numbers of slaves with an important alternative place to meet, to argue – and to plan. Many of the chapels, like their counterparts in Britain, were democratic forums where men of talent and abilities could emerge via their rhetoric, persuasiveness or simple appeal, to positions of prominence and influence in the community. And this was quite in addition to whatever interpretation slaves might put on the Christian messages placed before them. Self-esteem, self- and collective expression, images of a better life, the promise of future salvation, these and many other ideals and images had a radicalising effect on numbers of slaves. It is no coincidence that many of the slaves prominent in the revolts of 1816, 1823, and 1831 were members and leaders of their local chapels. By their lights, the slave holders had every reason to fear the missionaries.

The slaves who revolted in the early nineteenth-century British Caribbean were not primarily Africans; they tended to be local-born and were often skilled men enjoying what were traditionally considered to be better lifestyles within the slave communities. And cutting across this confused but volatile scene was the regular information, much of it garbled and inaccurate, about the British debate on black freedom. Planters were partly correct to argue that slave unrest must have been fermented by a pernicious alchemy of humanitarianism and missionary zeal. This is not to say that Christianity was radical; in many respects it was quite the opposite. Nonetheless its *social* impact in the British Caribbean was profoundly disruptive of the slave system. Whatever the *intentions* of its propagandists, the coming of non-conformity loosened the bonds of black slavery.

It is difficult to know what priority to give to black resistance. Clearly it was an inescapable feature of slave society; a ubiquitous response among the slaves which proved to be a crucial determinant in forging relations between black and white. On the whole, however, the very great majority of the millions of Africans dumped in the Americas resisted their oppression as best they could, not necessarily through violence, or trying to overthrow the system, but by trying to make as viable and decent a life – on their own terms – as circumstances would allow. They fended off the deliberate and haphazard blows of man and fate as best they could; fighting occasionally, but at other times grudgingly accommodating. But to see slaves as black human material, malleable to their owners' whims and needs is to ignore the remarkable scope and depth of black achievement in the teeth of hostile circumstances. Equally, to think of the slaves' reactions to enslavement in terms of simple alternatives – submission or resistance – is to overlook the diverse spectrum of human responses which black slavery elicited from millions of its victims.

8. The European Dimension

The history of black slavery in the Americas can be easily outlined; but much more elusive, though of great importance, is the position and role of Europe in the development, continuation and ultimate ending of slavery and the slave trade. Whatever forms bondage took before the European encroachment on West Africa, black slavery as it emerged in the Americas was called into being and perfected by Europeans. From the early days of white settlement, Europeans had come to look upon Africans as ideal instruments to pursue and effect European economic advancement. But to what extent Europe itself benefited from its involvement in black slavery is much more difficult to assess. At a 'commonsensical' level it might seem obvious and scarcely worth an argument that the Europeans *did* gain materially from black slavery. How could it have been otherwise in an economic relationship which persisted over such a long period of time and whose proponents fought so tenaciously to maintain the slave system? The problems remain: in what fashion was Europe a beneficiary from the slave system?

Europe's most immediately striking success was the development of the Americas. Without African labour, large tracts of the Americas could not have been developed in the form that they were. Caribbean and South American sugar, Brazilian coffee, Brazilian mining and 'King Cotton' – all were dependent upon Africans and their descendants. Doubtless other crops and economic systems would have evolved had white settlers and their European backers forgone the opportunity to use black labour. But they did not and that decision (which had a 'domino effect' in other areas of economic life) irreversibly changed the face of Africa, the Americas – and Europe.

The most immediate and obvious impact of slaving on Europe was to be found in the ports. The economic development generated by the slave trade was considerable, although the trade to and from Africa was not concerned uniquely with slaves. As with other areas of overseas trade, the initial requirements for equipping and despatching a slave ship (and later for founding the plantations) was capital. Men of business with surplus capital or access to friends and partners able to raise those funds, invested considerable sums in slaving voyages. Success bred success and slave traders and merchants who invested money in the slave ships ploughed their profits back into further missions. The result, in the case of Liverpool – the pre-eminent slaving port of the late eighteenth century – was a marked concentration of slaving interests in a small number of hands. The total amounts involved were, for the time, vast. By 1790 there was an estimated £1,088,526 tied up in Liverpool slavers and their cargoes.[1]

58. Strand Street, Liverpool

In other ports, where slaving was not as significant a local occupation, the pattern of local economic involvement tended to be quite different. In Whitehaven, for instance, there was an unusually wide spectrum of local investors in the local slave trade, including yeomen, widows, spinsters and even pawnbrokers and milliners.[2] Such diversity could be found in other countries. In the major French slaving port, Nantes, there was, as in Liverpool, an increasing concentration of capital in the slave trade; more and more slave ships controlled by fewer and fewer people, owners and investors.[3] While anyone with a ship to risk could gamble on the slave-trading venture, as the trade became more complex, the slave ships themselves changed, became more custom-built and hence involved greater capital outlay.

The capital cost of a slave ship was not the only major expense required of slavers. They needed, in addition, the goods used for barter in Africa. The drinks, guns, metalware, pottery and textiles used for those transactions were themselves an added stimulus to British, or other European, industry and trade. Trading houses, banks, merchants and entrepreneurs were all closely involved in the economic activity dependent on the slave trade. Whatever the risks and despite the occasional failure or disaster, the attractions of the slave trade were overwhelmingly seductive to all sorts and conditions of Europeans with an eye for profit or business. It would then be wrong to imagine that the sole instruments for the oppression of the slaves were the slave traders and slave owners; for there were many thousands of people whose involvement in slavery was crucial but less than direct. A parliamentary report on the Liverpool slave trade in the mid-1790s noted:

> This great annual return of wealth may be said to pervade the whole town, increasing the fortunes of the principal adventurers, and contributing to the support of the majority of the inhabitants; almost every man in Liverpool is a merchant, and he who cannot send a bale, will send a bandbox, it will therefore create little astonishment, that the attractive African meteor* has from time to time so dazzled their ideas, that almost every order of people is interested in a Guinea cargo.[4]

(* the slave trade)

The increasing concentration of the slave trade into certain ports, and then into ever fewer hands within those ports, was a general European phenomenon. Moreover, by examining the most obvious and important of slaving ports – London in the seventeenth century, Bristol early eighteenth, Liverpool late eighteenth century or Nantes late eighteenth century – we can easily overlook the *wider* maritime context. There were dozens of other ports with little or no interest in slaving. Yet for those ports which became slaving ports, there can be little doubt that their wellbeing was greatly enhanced by the slave trade.

Some indication of the impact of slave trading on certain European ports can be gauged from a number of surviving artefacts and architectural legacies which are derived from the slave trade. Large sections of the urban and dockside development of the slaving ports were, of necessity, dependent upon and in service to the slave trade. Similarly, merchants and shippers often built elegant homes and buildings from their successes in the slave trade just as returning planters constructed domestic monuments to the wealth and material

59. Broad Quay, Bristol, in the eighteenth century

achievements created by the slaves. Indeed the wealth of men with slaving interests became a commonplace in the mid- and late eighteenth century largely because the planters and merchants took pains to display and flaunt their slave-based wealth before their fellow countrymen at the spas, in the capital or, more substantially, in the form of their elaborate homes. Significantly many of these European buildings were suitably embossed with stone heads, carvings and representations of the negro. To this day these stone monuments are a reminder of the countless black victims who underpinned the wealth on which so much European extravagance was based.[5]

It would be wrong to try to describe the European involvement in slavery simply or even largely as a matter of profit or loss; there is no neat balance sheet which aptly describes the complexity of ties linking Europe to the growth of black slavery. In addition to the obvious economic considerations slavery had major social and political repercussions on Europe. At the human level, for instance, there were many thousands of Europeans who had a direct hand in and responsibility for enslaving and selling legions of Africans. Whereas government, monopoly companies and later private enterprise orchestrated the development of black slavery from the security and comfort of Europe's capitals and ports there were many thousands of Europeans more directly involved, often in dangerous and unpleasant fashions. This was particularly true, for instance, of

60. Negro faces as architectural decorations in eighteenth-century Bordeaux

the sailors who, if they survived, returned to the slave ports and their home towns with stories about Africa and the slave trade. Unusually large numbers of these men failed to survive, forming just one aspect of the fearful cost which Europeans thought justified in the headlong rush to pour black labour across the Atlantic. This particular and costly consequence of the entanglement with black slavery was only fully revealed in the late eighteenth century when humanitarians realised there was great political capital to be made from revealing it to the public, a clear feeling that the public would regard it as too high a price to pay.

In the short term perhaps the most noticeable facet of slavery's impact on Europe was the large number of blacks who found their way to Europe in the era of slavery. When faced by the African presence in European cities it was difficult to plead ignorance about the human consequences of the slave trade. Africans, as we have seen, had arrived in Europe long before the development of the slave trade, but it was the triangular trade which made possible substantial numbers of black arrivals in Europe. Indeed the first effective slave trade from Africa was to Portugal. Between 1450–1500 some 700–900 slaves were shipped annually to Portugal and even more were taken to the Madeira islands. In Portugal itself the slaves were sold in local slave markets and worked in a range of domestic and rural occupations. Inevitably as the slave trade grew in size, involving ever more European ports and, of course, growing numbers of Africans, numbers of slaves found their way to Europe. Some, like the early Portuguese slaves, went direct but increasingly Africans found their way to Europe via the slave trade itself. Those landing in European ports were sometimes the residue of an unsold cargo; others were sold in European cities as a bonus for returning sailors. Some arrived in the personal service of planters or government and military officials. Some went as sailors. But all were cast ashore as the human flotsam and jetsam of the Atlantic slave trade and with time their numbers grew, living in tightly knit urban communities (notably in the ports) though many others could be found scattered across the face of rural society where they worked as domestics.

The great majority of blacks in Europe had once been slaves in the Americas and their bondage did not end with landfall in Europe. Slavery was not merely encouraged in the Americas, but throughout much of the era of slavery it found a safe and hospitable home in Europe itself. The case of Britain is instructive. The first sizeable and consciously imported coffle of slaves was in 1555: 'certain black slaves, whereof some were tall and strong men, and could well agree with our meates and drinkes'. Official steps were taken to discourage such importations but, as Britain's slave colonies grew, so too did the number of blacks deposited in Britain, primarily in London.

Many of those imported as personal slaves (and who were openly sold in London newspapers) ran away to seek a precarious but independent life among the capital's teeming poor and were regularly augmented by fresh runaways who similarly found the temptations of freedom irresistible. Slave owners for their part complained, advertised for the runaways and occasionally turned to the courts for legal redress. In fact the legal problems posed by slavery in England were remarkably complex, yet despite those complications there can be no doubting the existence of slavery as a social institution in eighteenth-century England. Indeed it thrived. Englishmen bought and sold slaves in London; they bequeathed their slaves in their wills, shipped them back into the colonies and otherwise resold them abroad. In time the English black population, which seems to have been predominantly male, became quite sizeable; perhaps 20,000 by 1772 and posing the host society with a series of 'problems'. The complexity of black poverty, of miscegenation, of white hostility – all these and more helped precipitate intellectual and political debate about black slavery long before British abolitionists were able to whip up feeling against slavery in the last years of the century.

The legal complexities of slavery in England, and the wide publicity the cases received in the press, were important in keeping before the public gaze the difficulties faced by the black community and the moral and legal arguments about slavery and the slave trade. In the last quarter of the eighteenth century the British public, especially in London, were confronted by the undeniable human problems posed by slavery in the persons of the blacks who were overwhelmingly poor and were to be seen in and around the streets of the capital.

A modern researcher can easily come across surviving traces of these generally forlorn people, for their names and even their faces appear in numerous contemporary sources. They can be seen, for instance, in various prints and portraits, notably in portraits of families who employed black servants or owned slaves. Their traces also survive, though in less human form, in church records of baptism, marriage and death and also on headstones of their final resting places. Newspapers with their sprinkling of slave advertisements often provide other intriguing evidence. Best of all perhaps is the surviving work of a small band of black writers whose letters, tracts and political activities did much to advance the black cause in the late eighteenth century and which provides a unique insight into black society itself. By definition most slaves left few written sources, though this is less true of slaves in the US South where literacy and oral recollections form an invaluable entrée to slave life. In Britain and the British colonies the written memories of slaves are rare – but all the more valuable because of it.

There are then abundant sources about blacks in Britain from which we can reconstruct a useful picture of eighteenth-century black society. It was large, growing, and was widely considered a threat for that reason; its members often found sexual or family comfort with poor white women, to the chagrin of negrophobic elements in Britain and the colonies. Although the great majority were, like their peers in the Americas, labourers or domestics, many rose from unskilled origins to take up a range of skilled or unusual roles and tasks. We know of black boxers, musicians and entertainers, teachers, domestics, artisans and clerks; these and many more were all in addition to the poor and wretched blacks who haunted the streets of late eighteenth-century London.

61. Lady Portsmouth and her black servant, by Mignard

62. Sir William Young's family, by Zoffany

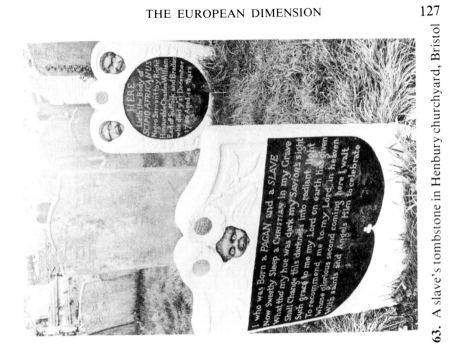

63. A slave's tombstone in Henbury churchyard, Bristol

64. Ignatius Sancho, Thomas Gainsborough's portrait of a prominent former slave in eighteenth-century London. Sancho's posthumously published letters provided invaluable insight into contemporary black society

65. A boxing match in 1822, cartoon by Cruikshank

66. 'Black, Brown and Fair', cartoon by Rowlandson (1807)

67. 'Lowest Life in London', cartoon by Cruikshank (1821)

As the black poor grew in numbers, there were concerted efforts to rid the capital of the 'problem' by persuading them to move to Africa. Most, however, had little desire to return to the slave-trading coast and Britain's black population, with all its attendant difficulties for the unhappy host society, only began to wither away when the slave trade was abolished in 1807 and slaves became too valuable in the West Indies to be carried into Britain. Yet, as late as 1834 there was a proposal in *The Times* to celebrate the ending of slavery in that year by a fund 'to build 12 alms houses for poor men and women of colour, in some spot on the roadside near the metropolis'.[6]

Africans and slaves could be found in abundance in other European countries which possessed slave colonies or had a hand in the slave trade. Africans were to be found in France as early as the sixteenth century but powerful political pressures built up in France to prevent the landing and settlement of slaves. When in 1571 a shipper in Bordeaux advertised slaves for sale, the local *parlement* declared slavery to be illegal, a ruling that was thought still to prevail a century later despite the fact that French colonies (where slavery was perfectly legal) were considered to be part of France itself.[7] After 1717, however, slave owners were allowed to keep their slaves in France though in 1738, in order to prevent the development of a black community, the duration a black could live in France was limited to three years. The reason was openly rascist; it was argued that black settlement gives 'the occasion . . . of the mixing of black blood in this kingdom'. To stop this, slaves were forbidden to marry in France. Nonetheless, they became sufficiently numerous that, between 1740 and 1750 it proved possible to raise a black military corps in France, though this was resisted by many. The numbers of blacks in France seem never to have been as high as in England (due largely to the different development of the respective empires and slave trades). Furthermore, in 1764 the French government forbade future black importations – slaves or free – arguing that such settlements resulted 'in a mixture that increases daily in France'.[8] This prohibition was enforced, but not entirely effectively. A new measure of 1777 reaffirmed the rule, offering similar fears as a justification:

> The Negroes are multiplying every day in France. They marry Europeans, the houses of prostitutes are infected by them; the colours mix, the blood is changing . . . these slaves, if they return to America, bring with them the spirit of freedom, independence, and equality, which they communicate to others.[9]

The same sentiments, in almost precisely the same terminology, could be found issuing from Englishmen and English planters at much the same time.

In 1778 a royal edict ordered all French slaves to be returned to the colonies or consigned to special stockades, though those with prior residence could register to stay (while still being forbidden to marry whites). But this, and all other issues to do with slavery and race, were soon to be engulfed by the all-consuming Revolution of 1789 which not only destroyed the old order in France but brought down the edifice of slavery in the colonies.

Among those blacks who settled in European cities and ports at the height of slavery, many secured their own freedom while some of their descendants even managed to become skilled and respected members of their communities. Others reached positions of some prominence and fame. The best remembered of blacks in Europe, however, were those famous in their own day as unusual objects of curiosity; remembered for their freakish appearance, unusual abilities or physical peculiarities. Such blacks who appeared on the stage and in fairgrounds, however, cannot disguise the fact that the very great bulk of the black population consisted of ordinary poor blacks with little to offer except their strength (as long as they had it) and, under the right circumstances, their colour; both factors, of course, being responsible for their enslavement in the first instance.

The colour of the Africans was not merely their most striking characteristic to white societies accustomed to perceiving the world in ethno-centric terms but, in time, it came to be offered as cause and justification for the enslavement of Africans. As we have seen, the prime motive for European enslavement of Africans was obviously (and self-admittedly) economic. With the passage of time, however, European writers began to justify the enslavement of Africans in terms of colour; suggesting that, in their blackness, the Africans bore the mark of Cain and were to be legitimately enslaved for that reason.[10] How many people believed such arguments is difficult to tell but there is powerful evidence, of varied sorts, to suggest the existence of a racist tradition in Europe which was nurtured by and found a particularly important focus in black slavery and the slave trade. It was hardly surprising then that those blacks who found their way to Europe in the eighteenth century should become victims not merely of the dehumanisation of the slave trade and slavery, but should find themselves, in Europe, confronted by openly racist antipathy.

The picture, as we might expect, is uneven. The history of slavery from the mid-eighteenth century onwards in Europe and parts of North America has to be set against the rise of humanitarianism; of individual and collective acts of assistance towards the blacks in an effort to modify and then to end the inhumanities of slavery. After all, the ending of the British slave trade in 1807 and of slavery itself in 1838 was (whatever the motives) primarily the work of British people in the metropolis. But this picture of brotherly philanthropy ought not to be overdrawn and needs to be offset by the deeply ingrained antipathy and hatred of blacks to be found on all hands in Europe. Of course, racism was not experienced by blacks alone. There were throughout the world (and, closer to home, in Ireland) vast numbers of indigenous peoples in colonial possessions who were regarded and treated as inferior beings by conquering and dominant European groups. This was as true of India as it was of Ireland; of North American Indians as it was later to be true of the native peoples of Australasia. As with the slave trade the European acts of conquest, domination and exploitation added to the emergent sense of superiority which, in time, blossomed into a fully grown racism which consigned native peoples to varied and graded levels of sub-species in the eyes of the dominant classes.

White Englishmen may in the early days of exploration have been merely curious about black people: by the mid-eighteenth century many believed themselves to be their natural, obvious and God-made superiors. Partly to maintain that superiority, many Europeans resisted black settlement in Europe which time and again was denounced as 'pollution' of European stock. In France it was feared that freed blacks 'might in great numbers come to live in the kingdom, mix with French blood by marriage and pass to their children their vicious tendencies'.[11] At precisely the same time an Englishman (admittedly with West Indian connections) denounced 'this mixture' which would, he claimed, 'spread so extensively as even to reach the middle and then the upper orders of the people, till the whole nation resembles the Portuguese and Moriscos in complexion of skin and baseness of mind'.[12]

It has been argued that the open racism so frequently expressed in mid- and late eighteenth-century literature – in tracts, magazines and newspapers – was unusual and was primarily the work of slave holders trying to justify and continue their possession of black slaves at a time when slavery was under attack.[13] In some respects this is true, but it tends to ignore the fact that slavery was an institution succoured by the most profound of racist arguments. And in the evolution of slavery a crucial role had been played by the active efforts of European rulers, governments and business interests, no less than the colonial authorities immediately in charge of the slave colonies.

68. 'The New Union Club', Cruikshank's caricature of abolitionists (1819)

It is also important to recall the open racism encountered daily by blacks living in Europe. In France they were rounded up and put into stockades. In England the government tried to collect them together and ship them to Africa. And at the personal level blacks faced daily rebuffs and insults far worse than those traditionally endured by the wretched and dispossessed. Insulted, assaulted, bought and sold, arbitrarily despatched (even when free) to the slave colonies, blacks were perpetually exposed to the pain and fear of arbitrary and capricious acts of malice and hatred. Theirs was a uniquely unhappy situation and the hostility and aggression shown towards them in Europe – both legacies of slavery in the Americas – were to survive long after the fabric of slavery itself had disappeared. Indeed the scars of black slavery are visible throughout the western world to this day.

9. Black Freedom

Slaves were themselves instrumental in securing a number of important freedoms within all slave societies. Indeed, as we have seen, the urge to freedom lay at the heart of much of the slave resistance so widespread in the Americas. The results of their efforts, however, were out of all proportion to the costs. There were, it is true, free blacks – notably the maroons – and individual runaways, who lived as best they could in a politically and geographically hostile environment. There were also numbers of slaves who were freed by their owners and who lived as free people in towns or on their own plots of land in the country where they survived as free though generally impoverished labourers and peasants. But such people were as physically isolated as they were socially untypical. They were, in effect, isolated free faces in a sea of slaves and though slave holders pointed to the slaves they had freed as an indication of their own altruism and as an indication of the rewards of faithful service, the existence of free blacks in slave societies was neither statistically significant nor was it an antidote to the all-pervading influence of slavery itself. For all the personal and collective urge for freedom among the slaves, the most effective effort to end the slave trade and slavery came from the non-slave forces, which were, more often than not, metropolitan.

This is perfectly understandable for, after all, slavery and the slave trade had been called into being by white European interests. And just as slavery itself cut across the lines of nationality, the movement to end it was similarly international. Yet the ending of slavery has aroused some of the fiercest of historical controversies and historians have disagreed more about the demise of slavery than perhaps about any other facet of its history. Before the publication of Eric Williams's seminal work, *Capitalism and Slavery* in 1944, historians tended to write of the ending of British slavery and the slave trade largely as a victory for the forces of morality over the entrenched interests of wickedness and godlessness (an interpretation close to the humanitarians' own view of their work). At its simplest, it was argued that the British, increasingly influenced by a growing evangelicalism, brought down Caribbean slavery because they found it to be offensive to their religious sensibilities. A parallel view might interpret the American Civil War as a crusade by a devout abolitionist North against the inhumanities of the slave-holding South.

Eric Williams, and countless historians since 1944, have sought to direct attention to the wider and perhaps more important economic considerations. To many modern readers it would seem inconceivable that a nation should end its commitment to an economically important institution (in this case slavery) simply because it was thought to be wrong or irreligious. Moreover, it is obvious that the change in attitudes towards slavery constituted a major upheaval. It is perfectly clear that by the 1820s and 1830s there were unusually large numbers of people in Britain who expressed themselves in favour of black freedom, yet this was manifestly *not* the case a mere fifty years before. Why that revolution in attitudes came about might go some way to explaining the nature and success of the fight to end slavery.

When the USA emerged from its colonial status to Britain in 1776 there were very few people on either side of the Atlantic who openly spoke out against slavery and the slave trade. Within the new USA, however, there was an obvious and unavoidable paradox, for those self-evident truths 'that all men are created equal' and were endowed 'by their Creator with certain unalienable Rights', notably 'Life, Liberty and the Pursuit of Happiness' did not apply to the slaves. The democratic revolution set in train by the Americans and, after upheavals in France, later to spread the ideals of modern democracy throughout the western world, hinged upon the 'rights of man'. Those rights, when argued in fundamental terms, were clearly indivisible and were applicable to all, irrespective of rank, age, sex or race. Indeed by the early 1790s democrats in England argued that the rights of man 'are not confined solely to this small island but are extended to the whole human race, black and white, high or low, rich or poor'.[1] Thus the age of democratic revolution planted the ideal of universal rights but in the USA where those rights had their practical genesis, they were soon brushed aside by the transformation in cotton production and the consequent demand for cheap slave labour. In the USA idealism rapidly succumbed to the onslaught of a contrary economic need. In Europe, however, such ideals seemed to be more influential, more obviously the case in France where one by-product of the 1789 Revolution was the destruction of French colonial slavery, most spectacularly, as we have seen, in Haiti. But there the price of black freedom had been appalling and the ruins of that once buoyant economy became an object lesson for all those (growing in numbers all the time) who took an interest in slavery. To slave supporters, Haiti offered a moral lesson of what happens when critics begin to tamper with and question the institution of slavery. Supporters of black freedom, on the other hand, felt that Haiti illustrated a quite contrary interpretation, namely that violence and destruction were an inevitable result of *not* improving and then ending conditions of black bondage. In truth the Haitian revolt was a phenomenon, like nothing before or since; a unique, unpredictable and unrepeatable cataclysm which was contingent on and a consequence of the better-known political upheavals in France.

Throughout the revolutionary upheavals of the 1790s Britain remained relatively stable and immune. Despite a resurgent democratic movement inspired both by France and the writings of Tom Paine, and notwithstanding the naval mutinies of 1797 and the Irish rebellion of 1798, Britain, compared with continental Europe, was relatively untroubled. Yet it was in Britain that major progress was made against the slave trade and slavery. There, from the 1760s, a campaign had been waged against slavery in England. The arguments advanced in that cause gained support as the dreadful details about slavery and the slave trade accumulated and received more and more attention. In this the Quakers and Methodists were particularly important, both drawing upon their contact with sympathisers in the Americas and winning to the cause the influential backing of their congregations across the nation. To add to their arguments, the plight of poor blacks in London, their numbers augmented by former slaves who had fought on the losing British side in North America, became a particularly pressing issue in the 1780s. Agitation on their behalf, the disastrous scheme to relocate them in Sierra Leone and the growing propaganda campaign all cumulatively established slavery as a major political issue in Britain. And all this took place even before the campaign against the slave trade was launched effectively in 1787. From small (largely Quaker) beginnings this drive swiftly developed into a massive, popular and nationally based movement. As it began to appeal to vast numbers of people throughout the country its strength and stridency surprised even its leaders.

The intellectual ideas behind the abolition movement can be traced to writers of the French and Scottish Enlightenment of the earlier eighteenth century and, of course, to the religious objections to human bondage advanced most notably by Quakers. By definition, however, such ideas were of limited direct influence and yet, shortly after establishing a committee to abolish the slave trade in 1787, the founding fathers were surprised at the support they could call upon. This was due in large measure to the successful

69. 'Anti-Saccharrites', Gillray's cartoon of the anti-slavery campaign against slave-grown sugar (1792)

HEROES OF THE SLAVE TRADE ABOLITION.

70. 'The Heroes of Abolition'. This nineteenth-century picture had no place for the slaves

tactics and propaganda, but it seems also to have been because abolition was nurtured by an older radical tradition reaching back to the campaigns of John Wilkes in the 1760s and 1770s and which had generated a reforming and humane sensibility throughout the country. People attached their names to anti-slave petitions in unprecedented numbers, and hundreds of those petitions arrived in Parliament demanding an end to the slave trade. Within Parliament abolitionists led by Wilberforce adroitly rallied MPs and ministers to their side.

Abolitionists expected the end of the slave trade to do more than stop the flow of Africans across the Atlantic, for they hoped that it would also force the planters to improve slaves' conditions, if only to encourage a healthier slave force to breed more successfully. Of course it was much easier to attack the slave trade than to defend it; it was always possible to find shocking stories and astounding statistics to speak against the slave trade. Research into the trade by Thomas Clarkson and accounts published by men experienced in slave trading regaled the reading public with an abundance of appalling and convincing details about the sufferings of the slaves. The West India lobby for their part tended to fall back on the arguments of economic utility: that the slave system yielded incalculable economic and social benefits both to the colonies and to the mother country and it would be folly to tamper with it merely for moral or religious reasons. Moreover, the planters had reason to feel confident in their arguments and recent research suggests that throughout these years the British slave system was indeed economically buoyant.[2] Nonetheless, more and more British people began to side with abolition, a trend accelerated after 1791 by the rise of plebeian radicals who added their weight to the abolitionist side. In addition, the cause could count on the growing numbers of churches and dissenting communities. Thus by the early 1790s the anti-slave trade campaign had become a major issue in Britain. A lot of public support was lost, however, by the mid-1790s largely because of the fears generated by the slave revolt in Haiti. But by then the abolition of the British slave trade was only a matter of time for within Parliament all that remained was to secure a few more MPs and Peers. It was purely accidental that the British slave trade was not abolished in the 1790s. It had to wait until 1807, delayed primarily by parliamentary and tactical factors, but in truth the country and the bulk of the politically influential had been won over to the idea of abolition a full decade earlier.

The British were not the first to abolish the slave trade. The Danes had led the way in 1802 following a series of reforming measures in Denmark (notably the ending of serfdom in 1785) but the Danish slave trade was much smaller than the British.[3] Economically the two societies were utterly different: Denmark an agricultural nation with an abolitionist monarch, Britain with a political system in which Parliament was supreme and undergoing the major changes we normally describe as the industrial revolution. And it is at this point that we must confront the arguments about abolition. Industrialisation was underpinned by an ideology more committed to free labour than slavery and this inevitably raises the question: did Britain abolish the slave trade because it was no longer considered important to a society undergoing industrialisation and committed, in increasing numbers of ways, to the practice of free labour? The evidence is confusing and current work suggests that at the time the British abolished the slave trade, the slave system as a whole was *not* in decline; indeed was accepted to be of continuing economic importance to Britain. Careful examination of the campaign to end the slave trade reveals very few traces of the presence of the new industrial order. Yet having said that, can it be purely accidental that the British ended the slave trade at the time of industrial growth?

Whatever answer we choose, there is no doubt that the ending of the slave trade, in 1807 had major repercussions on the slave societies of the West Indies, for slavery itself continued to survive for another thirty years. On some islands the populations were sexually uneven and therefore incapable of reproducing themselves like a 'normal' population. Hence the slave populations began to decline (as planters had said they would) and continued to do so until, in the 1820s, a more evenly balanced population began to mature and was able for the first time to establish demographic self-sufficiency. In the process, however, planters, faced with a shrinking labour force, were obliged to rationalise their labour operations, often obliging slaves who might have expected better, preferential tasks to undertake more arduous and gruelling work. This had the effect of compounding slave frustrations and angers at the time when news of the growing British commitment to black freedom was transmitted, normally in garbled fashion, back to the slave quarters. This in conjunction with the proliferation of the new chapels among the slaves helped the outbreak of slave resistance, notably the slave revolts of 1816, 1823 and 1831. News of the violence and appalling reprisals was brought back to Britain by returning missionaries who told of frustrated and antagonised black Christianity. It was scarcely surprising that by the mid-1820s the British public once more took up the issue of black slavery, urged in that direction by a revival of the abolitionist campaign. There followed a really remarkable outpouring of cheap or free literature; numerous and vastly attended lectures and the emergence of the question of black freedom as an issue in parliamentary elections. As before, slavery again became an important religious issue, especially among non-conformists, and the end result was that in the 1820s and 1830s the campaign for black freedom reached new and remarkable heights. Carried along by a wider demand for reform, of all kinds (factory, parliamentary and religious), the issue of black freedom was taken up by all ages, social groups and both sexes.

Anti-slavery became so powerful that the only restraint on abolitionist meetings was the physical capacity of the meeting place. It was, in effect, a crusade of quite extraordinary strength and which developed a dynamic of its own, persuading ever more people, of all sorts and conditions, of the iniquities and economic irrelevance of slavery. MPs and ministers were equally persuaded, and by the late 1820s it remained only a matter of time (and compensation) before the slaves in British possessions would be freed.

There is no doubt that in this last phase economic considerations became a notable feature in the political arguments. The West India lobby naturally persisted in advancing the view that slavery continued to be economically important. Among abolitionists there was a growing feeling, argued especially by men from the new industrial interests, that slavery no longer made economic sense in a society whose new persuasion was more committed to freedom: freedom of thought, conscience, trade and labour. It was still the case that the overwhelming bulk of abolitionist arguments – in print, private correspondence, in lectures and within Parliament – concerned itself with the immorality and irreligion of slavery. Nonetheless, it was politically useful and convincing to harness economic utility to morality. Thus slavery came to be seen as wrong and uneconomic. After prolonged public argument and parliamentary debate and wrangles, slavery in the British colonies was finally ended on 1 August 1838 (though some islands had ended it in 1834). Contrary to the fears of local whites, the three-quarters of a million slaves entered freedom peacefully. British slavery which had been born in and characterised by persistent violence came to a peaceful end.

The same could not be claimed for the USA. There the slave trade had been ended in 1807. In truth, however, the Atlantic slave trade was no longer necessary to the emergent USA since the local black population was remarkably fecund and able to reproduce itself and multiply. Up to the late eighteenth century slavery had rarely been as important in the mainland colonies as was manifestly the case in the West Indies and South America. This changed quite dramatically in the nineteenth century, as we have seen, with the revolution in cotton production. The western world began to wear cotton goods; cotton grown by slaves and manufactured by exploited textile workers. One consequence of this was that at the time the British had become overwhelmingly anti-slavery, the American South was developing a renewed appetite for slaves. These slaves were not provided by the Atlantic slave trade, however, but by local sources; whatever slave trade existed in the USA took place between and within states rather than across the Atlantic. In the northern states slavery had long ceased to have any economic importance and had effectively withered away before being banned by local legislation. In the North, among men of abolitionist sensibilities (who shared similar ideological and religious feelings with their friends in Britain) groups emerged who were keen to put an end to slavery throughout the union. But, swept along by the economic buoyancy created by cotton, the South was in no mood to yield to northern arguments about the morality of slavery. Slavery boomed and thrived on cotton. In 1810 there were 1,191,362 slaves in the USA and by 1860 it was about four million.[4] But as slavery blossomed in the South, so too did northern opposition to it, offering secular and religious objections. Many northern abolitionists were archetypically early nineteenth-century bourgeois and were unconvinced of the economics and morality of slavery. Unlike the British situation, however, the arguments between US abolitionists and the slave lobby were regularly scarred by acts of violence. Moreover, as the years passed and as, despite abolitionist efforts, slavery thrived, more and more Americans began to feel that slavery could only be ended by force. In the South a parallel seige mentality developed, largely encouraged by local newspapers; a feeling that the South would resist and that no compromise was possible with northern abolitionists. The end result was sharp divides separating the political communities on both sides of the Mason–Dixon line (though in truth the great majority of northerners were uninterested in slavery).

As we might expect US anti-slavery was sustained by a great variety of measures. The religious revival in the North focused on the sinfulness of slavery (much as early nineteenth-century evangelicals had done in Britain). Simultaneously the ideology of the industrialising North was unsympathetic to the notion of slavery in addition to which, the ending of slavery in the British Caribbean gave confidence to American campaigners, with men regularly crossing the Atlantic. If so important an institution as British slavery could be brought down in so short a time, there was every hope that the Americans might make similar progress. The Americans, however, faced a further three decades of struggle, with the

71. The war in America. Negroes in Savannah, Georgia in 1863

inevitable internal wrangles and disputes generated by personality clashes, regional and tactical disputes – and even differences between black and white abolitionists. Throughout the thirty years between 1838 and the 1860s there was an unmistakable wider process at work: 'the gradual but tragic erosion of understanding between North and South'. As this gulf widened, slavery itself prospered, yet, in the words of one historian, 'now so grotesquely at odds with the times'.[5] By mid-century there could be no doubt that slavery had become the most pressing political issue in the USA, dividing the nation primarily along sectional lines. The British had been able to offer a relatively united front about their own form of slavery because of geography; British slavery was out of sight, if not out of mind, 5000 miles away in the Caribbean. In the northern USA a powerful anti-southern feeling developed which focused on slavery, but which in fact was often espoused by northerners who had no tender feelings towards the slaves. Good and evil did not evenly divide along the Mason–Dixon line, though many contemporaries tried to suggest it did.

Lincoln's Republican win in 1860 (although in no way an anti-slavery platform) proved the final straw for the slave-owning South. There swiftly followed the tragedies of southern secession and Civil War; but it is salutary to remind ourselves that the Emancipation Proclamation was not issued until 1863.

Many people may find a certain irony here for, while it is true that there had been violent incidents in the South in the early nineteenth century, slavery in the USA, by comparison with Caribbean or South American slavery, had been remarkably peaceful. Yet US slavery was ended in the fearful violence of the Civil War whereas Caribbean slavery, punctuated – indeed characterised by – violence, ended in an utterly peaceful fashion. In truth they are incomparable historical situations given an apparent and deceptive similarity because both involved large servile black populations. Nonetheless, the facts offer a startling contrast. In the 1830s three-quarters of a million slaves in the Caribbean accepted their freedom peacefully whereas a quarter of a century later four million American slaves were granted their freedom only at the cost of America's most costly conflict.

Slavery in the USA was not alone in experiencing a revival in the nineteenth century for a similar story unfolded in Brazil and Cuba. Unlike the USA, however, both those countries' demand for slaves could not be satisfied by the local population. Consequently, and throughout much of the mid- and early nineteenth century the slave trade thrived across the Atlantic. One effect of this was that the British put enormous diplomatic and naval effort into suppressing

72. An anti-slave patrol attacking a slave ship

73. Burning slave barracoons

that trade. Foreign Office treaties supplemented by Royal Naval presence around the African coasts took up a great deal of time and effort. Yet despite those pressures the flow of Africans across the Atlantic continued – and would do so as long as the labour demands of Brazil and Cuba lured slave traders with their human cargoes.

There were some abolitionist successes in the early nineteenth century, notably as we have seen in the case of Britain and Denmark. The Dutch ceased slave trading in 1814 and the French too were persuaded to end their commitment to slaving. But as demand for slaves continued, the business of slave trading simply left the hands of the traditional slave traders and passed into new or revitalised interests: the Portuguese, Brazilians, Spanish and Americans. While the British took great pride in their own virtuous acts of abolition and insisted, in magisterial style that everyone should follow their example, their efforts have to be set against the statistics on the nineteenth-century slave trade. Philip Curtin has calculated that almost two million Africans were shipped across the Atlantic between 1811–70, the great majority going to Brazil and Cuba.[6] Abolitionist navies did intercept and free large numbers of African slaves who were then settled in the free experimental black societies in Sierra Leone and later Liberia, but these were small victories when set against the legions of Africans dumped in Brazil and Cuba.

74. Rescued slaves from a captured ship in 1873

It was surely no accident that for those Europeans who chose to end their colonial slavery in the early nineteenth century (excepting perhaps the British), slavery had become – or had always been – a peripheral issue. In 1836 the Portuguese ended slavery; Sweden in 1847; the Danes a year later and the Dutch in 1863. But in all these cases slavery played no significant role and the numbers of slaves were very small indeed. France posed a more complex problem and the quarter of a million colonial slaves were not formally emancipated until 1848 and only then as a by-product of the political convulsions which wracked France itself in that year.

In South America the problems of slavery and black freedom were inextricably associated with the wider issues of national independence. It is important to remind ourselves that the 'Age of Revolution', among whose basic principles was a growing commitment to national identity, had made its impact in South as well as North America. The revolutionary and Napoleonic Wars, for instance, had major repercussions throughout Spanish America. Peace in Europe in 1815 merely heralded fully fledged wars of independence in South America. Slowly but surely both sides in the region turned to local slaves to fight on their side, often in return for the promise of freedom. Thus the Spanish American Wars of Independence enhanced the status and importance of local blacks and gave them a role they would not readily forsake.[7] In addition, the ideology of national independence was itself corrosive of slavery; the ideals of political and human rights, however perceived, were of equal relevance and importance to the slaves of South America as they had been to the slaves in St Domingue in the 1790s. The ideas of the rights of man, however transmuted and whatever their setting, undermined not merely the structure of the old regime in Europe and South America, but pulled apart the very fabric of slavery itself.

Black freedom spread unevenly across the southern continent, most of the new republics freeing their slaves gradually. Moreover, that freedom often meant merely the replacement of a discriminatory class system for the old caste system. Yet at the mid-way mark in the nineteenth century black slavery survived on a major and secure basis only in Brazil and Cuba – and of course in the USA. In those three regions its survival had more to do with economic utility than with the weakness of local abolitionist pressures (though the two were often related).

Black freedom in the USA left Cuba and Brazil exceptional and isolated. Each, however, was sustained by a remarkable economic buoyancy – Cuban sugar and later tobacco, Brazilian sugar and later coffee. The result was, as with British slavery a century earlier, that local slavery was strong, economically significant and defended by powerful interest groups. However strong the local abolitionists, they were faced by a thriving institution. Growing Brazilian criticism

75. Negroes dancing in Reunion to celebrate the abolition of slavery

of local slavery began as a result of the international attacks (led by the British) on the Brazilian slave trade, a factor compounded by the impact of the US Civil War. By the 1870s the issue of slavery had entered into the intricacies of Brazilian politics and (like Britain in the 1820s) it was but a matter of time, manoeuvres and compromise before black freedom was conceded, however reluctantly, as a national measure. Even then, full black freedom was not declared until 1888: a full half century after British emancipation.

Cuban slavery had ended two years earlier but its history had been quite different. The importance of slaves to the nineteenth-century economy is revealed by the importations of Africans into Cuba. In the sixty years up to 1870 it has been calculated that more than a half million landed on that island.[8] But Cuba, no less than the rest of the Atlantic world, had been touched by the contagion of democratic ideals, although the distance from the centre of colonial power, in Madrid, tended to weaken the forces of Cuban liberalism and abolition. Moreover, and like Brazil, the example of black freedom in the USA had a profound effect on the Cuban and Spanish debate about slavery. By the end of the US Civil War, the issue of slavery was securely lodged as a major issue in Spanish politics, but it was the open rebellion and warfare in Cuba in the decade after 1868 which really loosened the fabric of local slavery. Like the wars of Latin American Independence before it, the Cuban fighting slackened the slave holders' grip at the very time when the arguments in Madrid about slavery had concentrated on the specifics of black freedom; about when and under what conditions black freedom could be granted. As with the Brazilian debate, the last twenty years of Cuban slavery took place to a growing awareness that slavery was ultimately a doomed institution – whatever economic role it might appear to play in the local scheme of things. It might be felt that such a view involved a hefty dose of retrospection unavailable to contemporaries. But there was a sense in which, as the nineteenth century advanced, black slavery throughout the Americas became ever more incongruous, not merely within its own immediate locale but within its wider hemispheric setting. As the commitment to black freedom seeped through the Americas and as more and more countries granted emancipation (whatever shortcomings that freedom might entail in practical terms) it proved difficult to argue for slavery on economic grounds against a growing tide of secular, political and ideological opposition.

Once again this brings the argument full circle. Is it imaginable that this major institution – so costly and apparently valuable in a number of different economic contexts – could have been ended by the power of humane and outraged sensibility which saw slavery as an intellectual and moral outrage? Or was slavery no longer suited to society's changing economic needs? The questions are more easily posed than answered. Furthermore, there is no easy way of disentangling economic factors from their wider political and intellectual climate. It seems likely that slavery, like other economic systems, depended for its wellbeing and survival not merely on the economic forces which created and then sustained it but, quite clearly, on a much broader social and political tolerance. The history of slavery in the nineteenth century is in large measure the story of the destruction of that tolerance and the creation of a social and political ideology throughout the western world which was utterly antithetical to slavery. The political climate undoubtedly changed and as it did so slavery struggled for its life. Thus, even when viewed in the rather bold and isolated contexts of economic rationality, slavery can be interpreted to have been economically viable in the USA, Brazil and Cuba in the nineteenth century and in the British West Indies before 1807; when in all those situations slavery was buoyant and profitable, it was a system which ironically was out of kilter with the times. In a world which talked increasingly of freedoms and rights and which saw in industrial progress unbounded material prospects (made possible in large part by the unshackling of free enterprise) an economic system which was sustained by contrary beliefs was both isolated and doomed. Moreover, the sense of slavery's impending doom is no mere retrospective judgement but one which was shared by growing numbers of contemporaries. Indeed it could be argued that this *sense* of slavery's inevitable decline and death was in itself a fatal malignancy which affected the wellbeing of slavery. Growing numbers of people, in colonies and metropolis alike, came to view slavery as anachronistic, irrational and wrong. And abolitionist organisations were able to campaign, with great political effect, and often at an international level, to end slavery.

We need not feel the urge to stress, however – as so many early historians clearly did – that this is an indication of a resurgent, virtuous morality, rooted in Christianity, overcoming one of mankind's greater acts of wickedness. After all, behind demands for black freedom there lay varied motives – of cynicism, racism, hatred and pure opportunism – all in full measure. Conversely it would be wrong to think of slave holders as people universally devoid of all morality or sensibility. Although slavery in the Americas involved a sharp racial divide between black and white, the virtues and vices among those contemporaries involved were not as evenly divided (though many abolitionists liked to think they were). While in retrospect few would argue that black freedom was not a major step towards greater humanity, the reasons which so often underpinned demands for black freedom were sometimes less than humane and altruistic.

Slave systems involved much more than the slaves and it is clear that the slave holders, like their black property, were as the nineteenth century advanced, anachronistic, able to survive only in a climate of ideological tolerance which had been created in an earlier age. Nonetheless, black slavery proved remarkably resiliant to attack. When it fell, it succumbed to a fatal combination of its own internal weaknesses and fierce onslaughts from its foes.

Notes and References

London is the place of publication unless otherwise stated, here and in the bibliography.

Chapter 1

1. M. I. Finley, *The Ancient Economy* (Chatto & Windus, 1973) p. 29.
2. Ibid., ch. 1.
3. T. Wiedemann, *Greek and Roman Slavery* (Croom Helm, 1981) p. 122.
4. Ibid., p. 123.
5. Ibid., p. 11.
6. Finley, *Ancient Economy*, p. 70.
7. Ibid., p. 71.
8. A. Andrewes, *The Greeks* (Hutchinson, 1967) p. 139.
9. Quoted in J. Ferguson and K. Chisolm, *Political and Social Life in the Great Age of Athens* (Milton Keynes: Open University, 1978) p. 64.
10. A. H. M. Jones, 'Slavery in the Ancient World', in M. I. Finley (ed.), *Slavery in Classical Antiquity* (Cambridge: Heffer, 1968) p. 3.
11. Ibid., p. 3; Wiedemann, *Greek and Roman Slavery*, p. 96.
12. T. B. L. Webster, *Life in Classical Athens* (Batsford, 1978) pp. 44–5.
13. Jones, 'Slavery in the Ancient World', pp. 4, 8.
14. Wiedemann, *Greek and Roman Slavery*, p. 45.
15. Andrewes, *The Greeks*, pp. 139–40.
16. H. D. Kitto, *The Greeks* (Penguin, 1960) p. 132.
17. Finley, *Ancient Economy*, p. 63.
18. Ibid., pp. 63–4.
19. Andrewes, *The Greeks*, pp. 139–40.
20. Wiedemann, *Greek and Roman Slavery*, p. 19.
21. Keith Hopkins, *Conquerors and Slaves* (Cambridge: Cambridge University Press, 1978) pp. 8–9.
22. Ibid., p. 9.
23. Ibid., p. 102.
24. Ibid., pp. 25–7.
25. P. A. Brunt, 'Work and Slavery', in J. P. V. D. Balsden (ed.), *Roman Civilisation* (C. A. Watt, 1965) p. 178.
26. J. Vogt, *Ancient Slavery and the Ideal of Man* (Oxford: Blackwell, 1974) pp. 44–5.

27. Wiedemann, *Greek and Roman Slavery*, pp. 215–22.
28. Hopkins, *Conquerors and Slaves*, p. 121.
29. Ibid.
30. Ibid., p. 123.
31. Ibid., p. 121.
32. Ibid., p. 115.
33. Finley, *Ancient Economy*, p. 89.

Chapter 2

1. James Graham-Campbell and Dafydd Kidd, *The Vikings* (British Museum Publications, 1980) p. 33.
2. H. R. Loyn, *Anglo-Saxon England and the Norman Conquest* (Longman, 1962) pp. 87–8.
3. R. H. Hilton, *The Decline of Serfdom in Medieval England* (Macmillan, 1970) p. 10.
4. Ibid., pp. 10–11.
5. Ibid., p. 14.
6. Perry Anderson, *Passages from Antiquity to Feudalism* (Verso, 1978) pp. 160–6.
7. .Ibid., p. 161.
8. Quoted in R. H. Hilton, *Bond Men Made Free* (Methuen, 1973) p. 54.
9. Ibid.
10. I. Origo, 'The Domestic Enemy', *Speculum*, xxx, 5 (July 1955).
11. Hilton, *Bond Men Made Free*, p. 58.
12. Ibid., ch. 3.
13. Hilton, *Decline*, p. 25.
14. Ibid., pp. 30–57.
15. Ibid., p. 56.
16. *The Wealth of Nations* (1776) book 3, ch. 6.
17. William Doyle, *The Old European Order* (Oxford: Oxford University Press, 1978) p. 96.
18. Ibid., p. 97.

Chapter 3

1. For these and other details see J. H. Parry, *The Age of Reconnaissance* (Weidenfeld and Nicholson, 1963) ch. 1.
2. Paul Edwards and James Walvin, *Black Personalities in England in the Era of Slavery* (Macmillan, 1983).
3. C. R. Boxer, *The Portuguese Seaborne Empire, 1415–1825* (Penguin, 1973) ch. 1.
4. P. D. Curtin, *The Atlantic Slave Trade, a Census* (Madison, Wisconsin: University of Wisconsin Press, 1969) p. 21.
5. Quoted in M. Craton, *Sinews of Empire: a Short History of British Slavery* (London and New York: 1974) p. 9.

6. Richard Hakluyt, *Principall Navigations . . .* (1589) 7 vols (Deutsch, 1926) vol. VII, p. 5.
7. Boxer, *The Portuguese Seaborne Empire*, pp. 111–12.
8. In M. Craton, J. Walvin and D. Wright (eds), *Slavery, Abolition and Emancipation* (Longman, 1976) p. 13.
9. Craton, *Sinews*, p. 44; H. Klein, *Middle Passage* (Princeton: Princeton University Press, 1978) p. 12.
10. Craton, *Sinews*, p. 46; Klein, *Middle Passage*, p. 12.
11. Willie Lee Rose (ed.), *A Documentary History of Slavery in North America* (New York: Oxford University Press, 1976) pp. 16, 22.
12. Bernard Bailyn *et al.* (eds), *The Great Republic* (Boston and New York: D. C. Heath, 1977) p. 45.
13. In Rose, *Documentary History*, p. 25.
14. Bailyn *et al.*, *The Great Republic*, p. 76.
15. Craton, *Sinews*, p. 46.

Chapter 4

1. The standard work on the demography of the slave trade remains P. D. Curtin, *The Atlantic Slave Trade, a Census.*
2. See J. E. Inikori, 'The Origins of the Diaspora', in A. I. Aswaja and M. Crowder (eds), *Tarikh*, 5, no. 4 (1978) p. 8.
3. See the debate on 'Indigenous African Slavery' in M. Craton (ed.), *Roots and Branches: Current Directions in Slave Studies* (Pergamon, 1979) pp. 19–83.
4. J. D. Fage, 'Slaves and Slavery in Western Africa, 1445–1700', *Journal of African History*, 21 (1980) 298.
5. In Craton *et al.*, *Slavery, Abolition and Emancipation*, pp. 38–9.
6. Walter Rodney, *How Europe Underdeveloped Africa* (Bogle L'Ouverture, 1972).
7. P. D. Curtin, S. Feierman, L. Thompson and J. Vansina, *African History* (Longman, 1978) pp. 227–31.
8. Ibid., pp. 237–8.
9. Ibid., p. 240.
10. Klein, *Middle Passage*, p. 3.
11. Ibid., p. 7.
12. Ibid., pp. 11–13.
13. See ch. 7 below.
14. Klein, *Middle Passage*, p. 16.
15. Ibid., p. 17.
16. John Atkins, 'Voyage to Guinea . . . (1735), in Craton *et al.*, *Slavery, Abolition and Emancipation*, p. 26.
17. Ibid., p. 33.
18. Quoted in Craton, *Sinews*, p. 85.
19. Craton *et al.*, *Slavery, Abolition and Emancipation*, p. 41.

20. Ibid.
21. Klein, *Middle Passage*, p. 236, n. 2.
22. Quoted in Roger Anstey, *The Atlantic Slave Trade and British Abolition, 1760–1810* (1975) p. 26.
23. Klein, *Middle Passage*, p. 229.
24. Anstey, *Atlantic Slave Trade*, pp. 30–1.
25. Craton, *Sinews*, p. 86.
26. Klein, *Middle Passage*, pp. 234–5.
27. Ibid.
28. John Atkins, 'Voyage to Guinea', in Craton *et al.*, p. 32.
29. 'Evidence of James Penny', *British Sessional Papers, Commons, Accounts and Papers* (1789) vol. XXVI, part 2.
30. Anstey, *Atlantic Slave Trade*, p. 32; James Walvin, *Black and White: the Negro and English Society, 1555–1945* (Allen Lane, 1973) pp. 92–3.
31. Anstey, *Atlantic Slave Trade*, pp. 32–3.
32. F. R. Augier and S. C. Gordon, *Sources of West Indian History* (Longman, 1967) p. 166.
33. Anstey, *Atlantic Slave Trade*, p. 26.
34. Klein, *Middle Passage*, p. 197.
35. Quoted in Curtin, *Slave Trade*, p. 282.
36. Augier and Gordon, *Sources of West Indian History*, p. 166.
37. Craton, *Sinews*, pp. 103–10.
38. Eric Williams, *Capitalism and Slavery* (Deutsch, 1944).
39. Ralph Davis, *The Industrial Revolution and British Overseas Trade* (Leicester: Leicester University Press, 1979).
40. Curtin *et al.*, *African History*, p. 213.
41. Seymour Drescher, *Econocide: British Slavery in the Era of Abolition* (London and Pittsburgh: University of Pittsburgh Press, 1977).

Chapter 5

1. Craton, *Sinews*, pp. 120–9.
2. Duncan Rice, *The Rise and Fall of Black Slavery* (Macmillan, 1975) pp. 266–73.
3. B. W. Higman, *Slave Population and Economy in Jamaica, 1807–1834* (Cambridge: Cambridge University Press, 1976) pp. 57–60.
4. R. C. Reinders, 'Slavery in New Orleans in the Decade before the Civil War', in E. D. Genovese and E. Miller (eds), *Plantation, Town and County* (Illinois: Illinois University Press, 1974) p. 369.
5. Ibid.
6. W. L. Richler, 'Slavery in Baton Rouge, 1820–1860', in Genovese and Miller, *Plantation, Town and County*, pp. 381–3.
7. T. Hershberg, 'Free Blacks in Ante-Bellum Philadelphia', in ibid.
8. Ibid., p. 439.

9. For instance, see Richard Wade, *Slavery in the Cities: the South 1820–1860* (New York: Oxford University Press, 1964).

10. E. Merton Coulter, 'Slavery and Freedom in Athens, Georgia, 1860–1866', in Genovese and Miller, *Plantation, Town and County*, p. 344.

11. Ibid., p. 349.

12. Ibid., pp. 352–3.

13. Leslie B. Rout Jnr, 'The African in Colonial Brazil', in M. I. Kilson and R. Rotberg (eds), *The African Diaspora* (Cambridge: Harvard University Press, 1976) p. 141.

14. Ibid., p. 152.

15. Ibid., p. 156.

16. Rice, *Rise and Fall*, p. 260.

Chapter 6

1. Higman, *Slave Population and Economy*, p. 168.

2. See in particular, E. D. Genovese, *Roll, Jordan, Roll* (Deutsch, 1975); R. W. Fogel and S. Engerman, *Time on the Cross: the Economics of American Negro Slavery*, 2 vols (Boston: Wildwood House, 1974); H. Gutman, *The Black Family in Slavery and Freedom* (New York, 1976).

3. Monica Schuler, 'Afro-American Slave Culture', in Craton, *Roots and Branches*, p. 131.

4. Ibid., p. 135.

5. See ch. 7 below.

6. G. E. Simpson, 'Religions of the Caribbean' in Kilson and Rotberg, *African Diaspora*, pp. 291–2.

7. John Newton, *The Journal of a Slave Trader* (Epworth Press, 1962).

8. Craton, *Sinews*, p. 213.

9. M. Craton, *Searching for the Invisible Man* (Cambridge, Mass.: Harvard University Press, 1978) pp. 54–5.

10. Ibid., p. 56.

11. Craton *et al.*, *Slavery, Abolition and Emancipation*, p. 8.

12. *Characteristic Traits of the Creolian and African Negro in Jamaica* (1797) (1976) p. 16.

13. Quoted in Walvin, *Black and White*, p. 70.

14. *Characteristic Traits*, pp. 17–18.

15. Ibid., p. 18.

16. Ibid., p. 15.

17. Craton *et al.*, *Slavery, Abolition and Emancipation*, p. 118.

18. Ibid., pp. 124–5.

19. Quoted in Genovese, *Roll*, p. 570.

20. Ibid., p. 572.

21. *Characteristic Traits*, p. 23.

22. E. Brathwaite, *The Development of Creole Society in Jamaica* (Oxford: Oxford University Press, 1971) pp. 229–30.

23. Genovese, *Roll*, pp. 576–7.
24. Ibid., p. 579.
25. Brathwaite, *Development of Creole Society*, p. 214.
26. Ibid., pp. 216–17.
27. Genovese, *Roll*, p. 196.
28. Quoted in ibid., p. 195.
29. M. Craton and J. Walvin, *A Jamaican Plantation, Worthy Park, 1670–1970* (London and Toronto, 1970) p. 135.
30. See, for example, Bryan Edwards's comments, quoted in *Slavery, Abolition and Emancipation*, pp. 73–4.
31. M. Craton and J. Walvin, *A Jamaican Plantation*, p. 135.
32. Brathwaite, *Development of Creole Society*, p. 236; Genovese, *Roll*, pp. 541–6.
33. Brathwaite, *Development of Creole Society*, p. 239.

Chapter 7
1. See, for instance, the essays in Stan Cohen (ed.), *Images of Deviance* (Penguin, 1971).
2. Genovese, *Roll*, pp. 599–612.
3. Ibid., p. 609.
4. *Gentleman's Magazine* (1788) pp. 1093–4.
5. Genovese, *Roll*, p. 609.
6. Barbara Bush, 'Defiance or Submission?' in *Immigrants and Minorities*, March 1982, vol. 1.
7. Genovese, *Roll*, p. 615.
8. Augier and Gordon, *Sources of West Indian History*, p. 168.
9. Brathwaite, *Development of Creole Society*, p. 157.
10. Ibid., pp. 157–8.
11. This argument can be seen in its starkest form in Orlando Patterson, *The Sociology of Slavery* (Macgibbon and Kee, 1967).
12. F. B. Smith, *The People's Health* (Croom Helm, 1979).
13. Quoted in Walvin, *Black and White*, p. 38.
14. Genovese, *Roll*, p. 588; Rice, *Rise and Fall*, p. 300. On the wider history of the slave revolts, see E. D. Genovese, *From Rebellion to Revolution: Afro-American Slave Revolts in the Making of the Modern World* (Baton Rouge: Louisiana State University Press, 1979); M. Craton, *Testing the Chains: Slave Rebellions and Other Forms of Resistance in the British West Indies, 1625–1838* (Ithaca, New York: Cornell University Press, 1983).
15. R. Price (ed.), *Maroon Societies: Rebel Slave Communities in the Americas* (Baltimore: Johns Hopkins University Press, 1980).
16. Leslie B. Rout Jnr, *The African Experience in Spanish America* (Cambridge: Cambridge University Press, 1976) pp. 100–4.

17. These and others can be found in Craton *et al.*, *Slavery, Abolition and Emancipation.*
18. R. Dunn, *Sugar and Slaves* (Cape, 1973) p. 312.
19. Rice, *Rise and Fall*, p. 74.
20. Ibid., 270.
21. Craton and Walvin, *A Jamaican Plantation*, p. 145.
22. Klein, *Middle Passage*, p. 13. For the history of the Haitian revolution, see David Geggus, *Slavery, War and Revolution: the British Occupation of St Domingue* (Oxford: Oxford University Press, 1981).
23. Klein, *Middle Passage*, p. 188.
24. Ibid., pp. 15–16.
25. Geggus, *Slavery, War and Revolution*, and Doyle, *Old European Order*, pp. 56–7.
26. A. Goodwin, *The Friends of Liberty* (Hutchinson, 1979).

Chapter 8

1. Anstey, *Atlantic Slave Trade*, p. 7.
2. Ibid., p. 8.
3. Ibid., pp. 8–9.
4. Craton *et al.*, *Slavery, Abolition and Emancipation*, p. 56.
5. Many of these are retained in a number of buildings in Bordeaux. See accompanying illustrations.
6. For the history of the British blacks, see Walvin, *Black and White*; Edwards and Walvin, *Black Personalities in England*.
7. W. Cohen, *The French Encounter with Africans* (Bloomington: Indiana University, 1980) pp. 44–5.
8. Ibid., pp. 110–11.
9. Ibid., p. 111.
10. W. Jordan, *White Over Black: American Attitudes toward the Negro, 1550–1812* (Penguin, 1969).
11. Cohen, *French Encounter*, p. 112.
12. Quoted in Walvin, *Black and White*, p. 54.
13. Anthony Barker, *The African Link* (Cass, 1978).

Chapter 9

1. The words are those of Thomas Hardy, founder of the London Corresponding Society. See James Walvin, 'The Propaganda of Anti-slavery', in Walvin (ed.), *Slavery and British Society, 1776–1846* (Macmillan, 1982).
2. S. Drescher, *Econocide: British Slavery in the Era of Slavery* (Pittsburgh: University of Pittsburgh Press, 1977).
3. See S. Engerman, 'Some Implications of the Abolition of the Slave Trade', in David Eltis and James Walvin (eds), *The Abolition of the Atlantic Slave Trade* (Madison, Wisconsin: University of Wisconsin Press, 1981).

4.　Rice, *Rise and Fall*, p. 292.
5.　Ibid., p. 327.
6.　Curtin, *Slave Trade*, ch. 8.
7.　Rout Jnr, *The African Experience*, ch. 6.
8.　Curtin, *Slave Trade*, p. 234.

Bibliography

This brief selection of books is designed solely to give non-specialist readers a guide to the more prominent, recent works in the field.

1 Slaves in Antiquity

M. I. Finley (ed.), *Slavery in Classical Antiquity* (Cambridge: Heffer, 1968).

——, *Ancient Slavery and Modern Ideology* (Chatto & Windus, 1980).

Keith Hopkins, *Conquerors and Slaves* (Cambridge: Cambridge University Press, 1978).

J. Vogt, *Ancient Slavery and the Ideal of Man* (Oxford: Blackwell, 1978).

J. L. Watson (ed.), *Asian and African Systems of Slavery* (Berkeley: University of California Press, 1980).

T. Wiedemann, *Greek and Roman Slavery* (Croom Helm, 1981).

2 Slaves and Serfs

Perry Anderson, *Passages from Antiquity to Feudalism* (Verso, 1978).

M. Bloch, *Feudal Society* (Routledge, 1961).

——, *French Rural History* (Routledge, 1966).

R. B. Dobson (ed.), *The Peasants' Revolt* (Macmillan, 1970).

R. H. Hilton, *The Decline of Serfdom in Medieval England* (Macmillan, 1970).

——, *Bond Men Made Free* (Methuen, 1973).

3 The Age of Discovery

C. R. Boxer, *The Portuguese Seaborne Empire, 1415–1825* (Penguin, 1973).

——, *The Dutch Seaborne Empire, 1600–1800* (Penguin, 1973).

J. H. Elliott, *Imperial Spain, 1469–1716* (Penguin, 1970).

J. H. Parry, *The Age of Reconnaissance* (Weidenfeld and Nicholson, 1963).

—— (ed.), *The European Reconnaissance* (New York: Mentor Books, 1968).

4 The African Diaspora

P. D. Curtin, *The Atlantic Slave Trade, a Census* (Madison, Wisconsin: University of Wisconsin Press, 1969).

—— et al., African History (Longman, 1978).

H. Gemery and J. Hogendorn, The Uncommon Market: Essays in the Economic History of the Atlantic Slave Trade (New York: Academic Press, 1978).

M. I. Kilson and R. Rotberg (eds), The African Diaspora (Cambridge, Mass.: Harvard University Press, 1976).

H. Klein, The Middle Passage: Comparative Studies in the Atlantic Slave Trade (Princeton: Princeton University Press, 1978).

S. Miers and I. Kopytoff (eds), Slavery in Africa (Madison, Wisconsin: University of Wisconsin Press, 1977).

5 Slave Work

M. Craton, Sinews of Empire: a Short History of British Slavery (London and New York: Temple Smith: Doubleday, 1974).

——, Searching for the Invisible Man: Slaves and Plantation Life in Jamaica (Cambridge, Mass.: Harvard University Press, 1978).

—— (ed.), Roots and Branches: Current Directions in Slave Studies (Toronto: Pergamon, 1979).

E. D. Genovese, Roll, Jordan, Roll (Deutsch, 1975).

—— and E. Miller, Plantation, Town and County (Illinois: Illinois University Press, 1974).

B. W. Higman, Slave Population and Economy in Jamaica, 1807–1834 (Cambridge: Cambridge University Press, 1976).

Duncan Rice, The Rise and Fall of Black Slavery (Macmillan, 1975).

Leslie B. Rout Jnr, The African Experience in Spanish America (Cambridge: Cambridge University Press, 1976).

6 Social Life

John Blassingame, The Slave Community (New York: Oxford University Press, 1979).

E. Brathwaite, The Development of Creole Society in Jamaica (Oxford: Oxford University Press, 1971).

M. Craton, J. Walvin, D. Wright (eds), Slavery, Abolition and Emancipation (Longman, 1976).

R. W. Vogel and S. Engerman, Time on the Cross: the Economics of American Negro Slavery, 2 vols (Boston: Wildwood House, 1974).

E. D. Genovese, Roll, Jordan, Roll (Deutsch, 1975).

H. Gutman, The Black Family in Slavery and Freedom (New York: Pantheon, 1976).

7 Resistance

M. Craton, Testing the Chains: Slave Rebellions and Other Forms of Resistance in the British West Indies, 1625–1838 (Ithaca, New York: Cornell University Press, 1983).

David Geggus, *Slavery, War and Revolution* (Oxford: Oxford University Press, 1981).

E. D. Genovese, *Rebellion to Revolution* (Baton Rouge: Louisiana State University Press, 1979).

R. Price (ed.), *Maroon Societies* (Baltimore: Johns Hopkins University Press, 1980).

8 The European Dimension

Roger Anstey, *The Atlantic Slave Trade and British Abolition, 1760–1810* (Macmillan, 1975).

A. J. Barker, *The African Link* (Cass, 1978).

W. Cohen, *The French Encounter with Africans* (Bloomington: Indiana University Press, 1980).

S. Drescher, *Econocide: British Slavery in the Era of Slavery* (Pittsburgh: University of Pittsburgh Press, 1977).

W. Jordan, *White Over Black: American Attitudes towards the Negro, 1550–1812* (Baltimore: Penguin, 1969).

J. Walvin (ed.), *Slavery and British Society, 1776–1846* (Macmillan, 1982).

——, *The Negro and English Society, 1555–1945* (Allen Lane, 1973).

9 Black Freedom

D. B. Davis, *The Problem of Slavery in Western Culture* (Ithaca, New York: Cornell University Press, 1966).

——, *The Problem of Slavery in the Age of Revolution* (Ithaca, New York: Cornell University Press, 1975).

D. Eltis and J. Walvin (eds), *The Abolition of the Atlantic Slave Trade* (Madison, Wisconsin: University of Wisconsin Press, 1981).

B. W. Higman, *Slave Population and Economy in Jamaica, 1807–1834* (Cambridge: Cambridge University Press, 1976).

Dale Porter, *The Abolition of the Slave Trade in England, 1784–1807* (Hamden, Conn.: Archon Books, 1970).

Eric Williams, *Capitalism and Slavery* (Deutsch, 1944; 1966).

Index